Who'd be a Minister's Wife?

Heather Tinker

Christian Focus

ISBN 1-85792-726-5

© Copyright Heather Tinker 2002

Published in 2002
by
Christian Focus Publications, Ltd.
Geanies House, Fearn, Tain,
Ross-shire, IV20 1TW, Great Britain.

Printed and bound by
Cox & Wyman, Cardiff Road, Reading

www.christianfocus.com

Cover Design by Alister MacInnes

Scripture quotations are from
The New International Version,
© 1973, 1978, 1984 by the International Bible Society

Contents

Dedication

To my family whom I love – Melvin,
Christopher, Michael and Philip, also Sophie
and the next generation of ministers' wives

Introduction

Hello, I'm Heather Tinker. I met my husband-to-be, Melvin, at Hull University – one of the best, according to that fount of all wisdom B.B.C.T.V.'s Blackadder when he said, 'Everyone knows the three great British universities are Oxford, Cambridge and Hull'. We were married the summer Melvin graduated. I was already a primary school teacher and he went on to teach biology at secondary level. Although he had an idea that he might one day go into full-time Christian work, we set up home as two teachers in Hertfordshire, little knowing that Melvin's future lay as a man of the cloth. During his three years teaching, God called him to the full-time ordained ministry in the Church of England and we left with our one-and-a-half year old son to go to live in Oxford for three years while Melvin trained. That was in 1980. Our quiver is now full and contains Christopher, Michael and Philip aged twenty-two, eighteen and thirteen at the time of writing. 'Blessed is the man whose quiver is full of them (children)' (Psalm 127:5). Over the years we have lived in various parts of the country and in very different circumstances.

I am writing this book expecting to make you laugh, cry and think, in the hope that you might find something useful to help you along the way in the situations into which God puts you. These are just my experiences and my views. You may not agree with them, but I hope that what you read will at least have the effect of making you think why you do what you do. I am no expert, just a Christian woman whose husband happens to be a minister, seeking to fulfil the tasks God has given me to the best of my ability. I pray that you will be able to do that too, and that despite our mistakes, when we go to glory God will be able to say, 'Well done, good and faithful servant'.

1

Expectations

Perfection

For some reason clergy and their families are not regarded as normal human beings. As children cannot imagine teachers having a normal life outside school, so it seems that clergy families are not thought to be normal either. When one of my sons was eight years old, his school friends seriously thought that we all slept on the pews in the church! Once, when I invited a mother to drop in for coffee at my house, she said, 'Oh, I don't think of it as your home, I think of it as the vicarage'. Such misconceptions produce ridiculous expectations, for example, that we are available at all times just sitting in the church waiting for someone to need us. People sometimes get quite annoyed when asked to ring back in office hours to book their wedding. Then there are those who ring up to book 'the christening' just when I am about to go over to the church for the morning or evening service and cannot understand why the vicar isn't there for them!

People don't seem to think we are ordinary flesh and blood with normal human characteristics. A young lady once said to me, when I told her my husband was not in church because he had flu, 'You don't think of the vicar being ill, do you?' Well I do! Then on one of the many occasions when one of my normal children had a tantrum on the doorstep, the observation was made, 'Oh, I'm glad your children are naughty too'. What *did* she expect? Ecclesiastical people can be just as strange in their thinking. A bishop's wife who called round for some reason asked how my children were. She was surprised to discover that they were quite well as several clergy children in the diocese had the chickenpox. As we don't frequent the same neighbourhoods I would not have expected any connection, but she seemed to think that there was some sort of bond between the families whereby we could even pass on infections over a distance!

Extraordinary human beings

Even other professionals seem to have problems in seeing us as ordinary people. I had been to the doctor and needed to be referred to a consultant. At the hospital I saw the letter she had written. It began, 'Dear So and So, This vicar's wife...' I still cannot see what relevance my husband's occupation had to the state of my bowels! I could not help thinking that she would not have dreamt of writing 'this painter and decorator's wife....'. What is it with ministers and their families? I suppose the only answer is to be normal and to keep mixing with the community until people eventually cotton on. But many will inevitably carry on with their impressions, no doubt gleaned from caricature vicars and their wives of the inept type that we see on TV soaps and sitcoms.

People say that living in the manse or vicarage is like living in a goldfish bowl, everyone can see in from all sides and know exactly what we are doing. It certainly feels like that at times. When we have lived in a house on a street next to other houses in a row, we have felt less exposed than when the vicarage has been on site. Even so, everyone knew it was a church house and had their expectations of what we were going to be like and how we and our children should behave. I heard of a clergy family who were accused by neighbours in a letter to the church authorities of 'lowering the tone of the neighbourhood'. The chief moan seemed to be that they had children and that they didn't keep the garden in sufficiently good order. They admitted to not being great gardeners, but they were careful at least to keep the lawn mowed!

God never promised Christians an easy time. In fact Jesus says to us, 'Woe to you when all men speak well of you, for that is how their fathers treated the false prophets' (Luke 6:26). If our husbands are teaching the Bible clearly then many will not like it, and the less scrupulous will say all sorts of nasty things about them. Rumours will be spread, lies told and attempts made to undermine their ministry. If we are experiencing such things it is probably a good sign, because the devil doesn't like the Word of God going out and he will do all he can to stop it. Of course it is not only the messengers who suffer, but also we who love them and share our lives with them. It doesn't make the experience pleasant to know this, but it does give meaning to it and therefore helps us to cope in God's strength. James exhorts us to, 'Consider it pure joy, my brothers, whenever you face trials of many kinds, because you know that the testing of your faith develops perseverance. Perseverance must finish its work so that you may be mature and complete, not lacking anything' (James 1:2-3). It is only when our faith is tested that we find out how real it is, and this is true for our children too.

Superwoman

Sometimes we meet an assumption that we have been theologically trained along with our husbands. A few will have some sort of training, but most of us haven't. The congregation presume that we have been given special gifts to make us into ministers' wives and that we are super-spiritual with no problems – just like him of course! They believe that we won't ever suffer from doubts or be anything but loving and patient. I often think that if we didn't tend to live in detached houses the neighbours would be able to testify to the fact that this is not true because they would hear us when we shout at the children. The assumption is that we will take everything in our stride, that we don't hurt, feel lonely or vulnerable. It comes as a surprise to people when they find out that we do.

I can remember when my eldest son went off to university. I was pleased for him to go as I knew it was good and right. However, although I know that it's our job to help our children to grow up into independent adults, I cried on and off for a week. I shut his bedroom door because I couldn't bear to see it empty and so tidy! People asked me how he was and I couldn't hold back the tears. One lady was particularly struck that I was upset (and therefore normal) and commented on the fact. It helped her to see me as a fellow human being and she related to me better after that. I don't quite know how we overcome this problem because we can't really go round wearing our hearts on our sleeves. That would be both difficult and inappropriate. In a sense we do need to be strong because weak people can't lead effectively. Somewhere there must be a happy medium; confident enough to lead, but vulnerable enough to show our shared humanity.

Tremendous expectations may be had of the wife of the new minister, of the roles she will take on and the work she will do, although this may be changing . She may be asked to speak at meetings, and not just at her own church as word seems to get round the grapevine that there is a new minister's wife in town! When approached, I've politely said that I don't 'speak'. I don't mind leading Bible studies because they are informal and everyone is encouraged to join in and I don't have to do all the talking, but I'm terrified at the thought of standing up in front of people and speaking for half-an-hour even though I am a teacher by profession. It's not the standing up, but I don't think I could keep speaking and sound interesting for that length of time. Requests may, however, lead us to think about new spheres of service into which God might be leading us. Just because I have not felt able to do a particular thing before, shouldn't mean I can never do it. I don't know about you, but I am often encouraging others to be open to new ventures. I need to be aware that this might apply to me too.

Then there are the groups in every new church who would love the minister's wife to join, preferably to take over and run the meetings for them, but how it has always been done, of course! Have you noticed that often when new ideas are suggested, they are met with one of two reactions; either, 'We've always done it this way' or, 'We've tried it that way before and it didn't work then, so it won't work now'. The result is sanctified inertia! When confronted with all the groups I could join in a new church, I have always taken the line, 'I'm just settling in and not making any commitments yet. I'll see how things go.' As it is not possible for one person to be at everything, we have to prayerfully make up our minds, asking ourselves questions. Which groups can I serve well? Which will I fit into best? How many can I reasonably expect to be part of given my other responsibilities? It will be helpful for the church members to see our limitations and individuality.

Ordinary women

One thing we can all do to help this situation is to prepare the people at our church as we come up to the time to leave. We can find replacements for the jobs we've been doing in order that there are no gaps the new minister's wife is expected to fill, and we can teach the people not to have preconceived ideas about what she might want to do. If the congregation is able to do so, it is better for them to run things themselves anyway and not rely on the minister and his wife to do everything. Of course, the next minister may not have a wife and then they would be stuck!

There still seems to be some expectations of our creative abilities, particularly amongst the older members of the congregation. But this may be fading because younger generations can't make things either! I am hopeless at flower arranging. I did go on a workshop on the subject once, but I am still hopeless. I see that a firm will now deliver a flower arrangement in a vase for you, so that a beautifully arranged bouquet isn't ruined as soon as we try to put it into a vase at home.

I have had some success at banners though, which took me by surprise (a definite guiding hand by the Holy Spirit there I think). Perhaps we need to be positive and offer what we *can* do to compensate for what we cannot do.

Something Melvin and I have learned is that while we cannot give everyone everything they want, manageable means can be found to help people feel wanted. For instance, we now have a 'senior members of the congregation' coffee morning once a term. Tactfully we let them decide for themselves if they are 'senior' or not! We invite them all along to the vicarage where they meet others they have known for many years but hardly ever see nowadays because they attend different services on a Sunday. They chat away, have a great time and are touchingly grateful at the end. What is more I make an extra effort to bake scones, biscuits and mince pies for appropriate seasons. Fortunately I can cook and they always commend me on my scones and my pastry. There may be many things I can't do, but I can bake.

Another idea we have tried is to have a newcomers' meal once a term. This has been very successful in helping people feel welcome and it helps them to get to know each other. It is an effective way of welcoming several people at once and, providing the menu is kept simple but tasty, it shouldn't be too much of a burden. At first we had soup for a starter, but I soon abandoned that idea as it was too complicated, not least because I haven't got enough pans or gas rings on the cooker. For the main course I make two large saucepans full of different meat or vegetarian dishes. For instance, turkey and mushroom, pork and orange or chilli con carne. That gives people a choice. Then I serve rice (no peeling!) and two vegetables. That has always gone down well. For sweet I make a fresh fruit salad, which is easy, and for the less waist conscious I serve a choice of previously frozen gateaux and cheesecakes from the supermarket. Something in me feels that is cheating because dishes ought to be home-made, but people actually feel indulged (especially the men!), and it does save a lot of work. We serve a fruit punch made up of 2 litres of lemonade, 1 litre of pineapple juice and 2 litres of orange juice mixed with slices of orange added. Again it's very simple, but effective. As the whole meal comes to about £1.50 a head the church can afford to reimburse us. We aim to invite ten or twelve people, making it up to fourteen with us. I find that a reasonable number to cater for. The guests would be a mixture of old and young, marrieds and single. I say 'aim' to invite, because Melvin forgets who he has invited and it has been known for us to think everyone has arrived when the door bell rings and there is another couple on the doorstep. Then he remembers! That is where casserole type dishes are useful because they are expandable.

People, especially the elderly, like us to be at *their* meeting and visit them at home. It is impossible. Our current vicarage has a flat attached where the housekeeper lived. She would have not only kept house (and maybe had a husband who looked after the grounds), but she would have prepared food for the vicar's wife to take to the poor, leaving her free to do her good deeds without having to carry out domestic chores for the family. The other point of course is that in the old days the population of parishes was so much smaller than nowadays (we have over 20,000 in ours) making it more reasonable to know everybody. I handle this problem with the above coffee mornings, a few strategic visits and taking every opportunity for the casual chat. For example, if I see someone in the street I take an extra few minutes to walk along with them and talk. Then they feel I have visited them. Unfortunately some will never be satisfied, but that cannot be helped. We and our husbands have to decide what our priorities are and use our time accordingly. Because we see the building up of Christians and evangelism as our most important tasks, I want the activities I choose to take part in to reflect this. Preparing and leading a Bible Study would therefore take priority over tea and a casual chat.

Handling criticism

This brings us to the subject of handling criticism. Clergy couples are bound to be criticised. Jesus was. 'At this the Jews began to grumble about him ...' (John 6:41). The apostles got their fair share of criticism and so will we, in fact, as we have seen already there is something wrong if we don't. Jesus warned us, 'Woe to you when men speak well of you, for that is how their fathers treated the false prophets' (Luke 6:26). Some people won't like what we teach from the Bible. I think they sometimes take out on the minister their feelings about God, seeing him as God's representative. Apart from criticism which stems from the offence of the gospel, we'll get it because organisationally and personally we are not perfect, nor will we do everything the way each individual in our church would want us to.

Our husbands will probably get more criticism than we do, but people may use us to convey it. Anyway, we are in the ministry together as married couples and what affects them affects us. Melvin and I have always found letters the most difficult kind of criticism to take. The trouble is that letters don't smile: there is no body language with them. I know of churches where people are in the habit of writing letters when they want to say something. They might give in their letter just before a service or put one through the letter-box as their minister is about to go on holiday, probably without realising that by doing this they cause maximum disruption to the ministry and to their minister's much needed breaks. I suppose it is part of the mentality that sees the clergy, not as human beings with their own needs, but as servants (which we are, in a sense, but not slaves), simply there to meet the needs of other people.

It could be argued that a minister will not be there for very long if his needs are not met, because he will not be able to keep going. Letters such as, 'I am withdrawing from the mother and toddler group leadership forthwith as we are leaving the church. Yours ever......' That's it! I am left wondering who is going to lead the toddler group tomorrow and why they are leaving the church. Imagination sets in then - avoid imagining at all costs!- and I can come up with some amazing reasons and cause myself much unnecessary heartache. Ministers and their wives need to keep each other rooted in reality and try to find out the real reason as soon as possible. Then there is the person who had raised something with you which you thought you had resolved together, but you find a letter on the mat the next day which ruins your day off. Moral - I suggest never reading letters just before a service or during time off and don't let anyone 'just have a quiet word' at these times either. It may be good news, but it may not, and the risk is too great. Let it wait.

When you do get criticism, weigh it up. Who does it come from? Have they the standing to say what they've said? Are they worth listening to? Is it valid? If it is, then pray and do something about it. If it is not, then put it to one side. Something Melvin does now is to keep all the encouraging letters and cards he gets in a file and when he needs to counteract hurtful criticism, or just needs a boost, he can get the file out and be heartened. It is so easy to let one negative outweigh ten positives. We need to encourage each other to keep on. 'Therefore encourage one another and build each other

up, just as in fact you are doing'
(1 Thessalonians 4:18).

We can't please everyone, nor should we,
and we can't do everything either. There
are awkward people around and obviously
the best answer is for God to convict and
change them. We need to commit them to
the Lord, asking him to help us to cope
meanwhile with whatever difficulties they
cause us. We are not alone, we have our
loving heavenly Father and we have our
Christian friends to help us. We must never
let our pride cause us to feel we should be
successful on our own; that somehow we
have failed if we need help. After all, the
apostles needed each other. When things
went wrong they helped each other. We are
merely God's servants, not greater than our
master who needed his friends too. Let us
not be foolish and try to go it alone.

The show must go on

What happens when your husband, the
leader of the church congregation, is taken
ill? I find this quite a difficult time. First of
all no-one likes it when their nearest and
dearest is ill, particularly when it's serious. I
have to watch him suffer, when there may
be little I can do to help. My 'other half' is
not there to give me what I need and I have

to manage without his practical and emotional help. There is no encouragement from him and it can feel very lonely. But while I'm coping with my personal life, I also have to think about the organisation of which Melvin is in charge. I can't just ring into the office and leave it to the company to sort out his responsibilities. I'm aware of the needs of a group of people whom we love and care for and whom we do not want to let down. Obviously if my husband is going to be out of action for any length of time I have to inform the powers that be. But for a short while, I try to keep things going myself; and I don't always know if an illness is going to be long-term or not.

What do ministers' wives do when their husbands are ill? There will be differences according to what the set up is and whether he is on his own or there are others on the staff team, and how big and complex the operation is. If it is big there will be more staff, but then there is more for your husband to lie in his bed and worry about! In my experience it is very difficult for him to stop thinking about work. Living on the job obviously makes it more difficult, and even when he's unwell I find it very hard to keep Melvin out of his study, to stop him answering post or e-mails or 'just seeing to something'. I wonder whether I should tape up the study door! Some time ago, when he had been ill enough to have been hospitalised, I found he had sneaked into his study and opened his post! I was going to open it and filter out what he could harmlessly look at, but hadn't got round to it. He just couldn't wait!

When Melvin is ill, in order to keep him from working I have to make phone calls to his colleagues and others with messages, whilst at the same time keeping the family going and tending to his needs. Consequently, by the time he is better I find myself exhausted and reckon I need a few days off to recover my own strength! Fortunately 'I can do everything through him who gives me strength' (Philippians 4:13).

It's lonely at the top

Ministers of church fellowships carry responsibility under God for the working of the organisation and the care of the members. They may work with a team of other paid ministers or elders/church officials appointed by the church, but if the buck stops with them, then they are 'at the top'. This may seem to be in contradiction to their calling to 'serve', which is of course what 'ministry' is all about, but I think the position is akin to ministers of state, or indeed the

Prime Minister of the country. They serve the people with the help of a team, but they alone are responsible for how things are run and can be called to account if anything goes wrong. Similarly, ministers of the church can feel very lonely in the responsibility they carry on their shoulders. I think that this may be even heavier than in the secular world, because the eternal destiny of those in their care is at stake. Of course, God alone saves and sanctifies, but he has strong words to say about those who do not teach the people properly. 'If the watchman sees the sword coming and does not blow the trumpet to warn the people and the sword comes and takes the life of one of them, that man will be taken away because of his sin, but I will hold the watchman accountable for his blood' (Ezekiel 33:6). 'And the devil, who deceived them, was thrown into the lake of burning sulphur, where the beast and the false prophet had been thrown. They will be tormented day and night for ever and ever' (Revelation 20:10).

One thing we have found difficult in the position we hold is keeping and making friends. It was quite different when Melvin was a curate (assistant or trainee minister) and we noticed a big shift in the way we were viewed by the congregation when he became a vicar (i.e. the man in charge). As the curate and his family, it seemed we were seen much more as 'one of us'. I am not sure what made the difference. It may have been our age, as we were much younger then, but I think it has more to do with status. However people value our ministry, we are still the boss and his family. Some will put us on a pedestal, others will hold us responsible for all the problems. Either way we may be seen as remote. This makes it a lonely life in terms of relationships. When we're in an assistant role, people see us as equals and are more relaxed with us and more sociable. It is not that anyone has been rude since Melvin became a vicar. People are friendly and chatty, but with many there seems to be a certain distance. In coming to terms with this we tried to think back to the dim and distant past when we were ordinary members of a church. We did hold the minister in awe. We once had one round to tea, but we weren't as at ease as we were with the curate and his family. We would never have dared to tell the minister that we thought his sermon was good - it just wasn't our place, though we know now how important any word of encouragement is to the preacher.

Thus it is difficult to make friends within the congregation. Some say that we shouldn't try. They say it is too risky as we will cause feelings of jealousy and suspicion amongst those we don't befriend as to what secrets we might be sharing. Some clergy couples have had experience of people trying to worm their way into their favour for one reason or another, even offering financial gifts. This is dangerous and to be resisted. Acceptance could bring about an embarrassing position or the temptation to compromise on what is right and best for the church in order to please an individual. As a result some feel that their only friends can be other clergy.

If we know ministers and their wives who share our theological position and therefore are in the same business as us, and with whom we get on personally, then their friendship is easy and valuable. They understand our situation and they are good to talk with about anything. I have discovered that old friends are increasingly precious as we go on in the ministry. They often have a healthy view of us, giving us no airs and graces. They are also out of the immediate situation. Unfortunately, we find it more and more difficult to keep up with friends as we have moved around the country. Distances between friends can be great and we don't have many weekends off in a year. So it's easy to lose touch with those who cannot be visited in a day, unless they are willing and able to travel to us. The telephone is a wonderful invention and helps to reduce that sense of distance, but I think we need to meet up sometimes to keep relationships going.

We have found that our best friends are each other. Sometimes it feels as though only we really understand where we're at and what we're going through. There have been times when we have cuddled up in bed at night feeling very alone in the ministry, apart from God of course. Clergy couples have each other, which is wonderful, and we should guard our marriage relationship with all we have.

2

Children

The choice about childbearing

Nowadays we have choice about trying to have children. Some would argue from Genesis that children should be a natural part of a Christian marriage, i.e. that we should expect to have children unless there is a medical reason why we cannot. Some would argue further that we should take the children God gives us without the use of contraception. However, most Christians would say that we may use advances in medicine to regulate our families.

There was a useful little book published in 1985 in a series associated with *Christian Woman* magazine called *Family Planning*. In her conclusion, Gail Lawther says: 'We have seen that sex within marriage is a part of God's good plan for humankind, and that it is not right just to restrict it to procreation.

Every couple has the justification if they choose, to enjoy this part of their marriage without a constant fear of pregnancy. Contraception is one of the factors that makes this enjoyment possible. There is no biblical argument which prohibits the use of contraception. The thoughtful use of contraception also helps to protect the health of the woman between children, and the health of subsequent children. It also helps the couple avoid the emotional, financial and even spiritual strains of conceiving a child too soon or at the wrong time. From the point of view of Christians as world citizens, it also helps to keep a small check on the national and worldwide population level.'

How does a couple decide how many children they should have? I suppose it will depend on many factors such as age and health; what number would be reasonable considering the type of housing you might expect to have or the size of car you can afford, quite apart from your abilities to cope with little (becoming bigger) individuals all needing your separate attention. We must know our limitations for the sake of ourselves, our marriage, the other children and everyone else we come into contact with.

Romans 12:2 states 'Do not conform any longer to the pattern of this world, but be transformed by the renewing of your mind.

Then you will be able to test and approve what God's will is - his good, pleasing and perfect will.' I think this tells us to use our God-given brains to think issues through for ourselves rather than accepting what others do, even if they are Christians. We should do what is right for *us*. Christians should have better reasons for doing things than 'keeping up with the Joneses'. Sadly there will be those reading this book who long to have children, but are unable to do so. I have seen the sorrow this causes, and to them I offer the truth that applies to all the situations we grieve over, 'We know why we trust God who knows why' (Os Guiness in his book *Doubt*).

Tough blessings

Children are a blessing from the Lord, a reward from him - it's official, it's there in the Word of God. 'Sons are a heritage from the Lord, children a reward from him' `(Psalm 127:3). Remember that next time you are there in the middle of a toddler tantrum or a loud argument with your teenager. I have come to the conclusion that toddlers and teenagers are much the same, only the latter are bigger! They both assert their independence, they both scream and shout and are unreasonable. The differences are that toddlers, who have less vocabulary but equal lung power, just lie on the floor to scream whereas teenagers batter you with words and, when that fails, slam doors and stamp around the house. If the walls survive the toddlers throwing things, it's to be hoped the door frames will survive being slammed (you could ask for the glass-panelled doors to be toughened in advance!). One of my toddlers would talk to the wall for solace and another enjoyed throwing his toys around until he realised that they were breaking on impact and he soon wouldn't have any left! What about reasoning with them? I have tried that all the way along - toddlers don't grasp the concept, they only know what they want, and teenagers just keep repeating their views *ad infinitum*. I suppose they hope some sort of erosion will take place. I give up now after stating my case, (which is unacceptable whatever my reasoning might be because it is just not what is wanted,) and walk away. Eventually they come round– you just have to be patient.

The Bible is very keen on discipline. Solomon in God's wisdom said, 'Discipline your son, for in that there is hope; do not be a willing party to his death' (Proverbs 19:18). Having now had teenagers, I am so pleased that we took the time and effort to exercise proper discipline when the boys were smaller than us. It has certainly paid off now, as even though they sometimes feel obliged to shout and scream, in the end they do what we ask as they have been brought up to do. They even tell other adults that they respect us, and that is lovely to hear. So it may be hard work and not what many around us are doing, but it is worth working at discipline for your sake as well as theirs. Ultimately, our children will function so much better as adults and be of more use to God.

It goes without saying that discipline must be alongside love. Dr Ross Campbell in *How to really love your child* says, 'We can be confident that a child is correctly disciplined only if our primary relationship with him or her is one of unconditional love. Without a basis of unconditional love it is not possible to understand a child, his behaviour, or to know how to deal with his misbehaviour. Unconditional love can be viewed as a guiding light in child rearing. Without it, we parents are operating in the dark with no daily landmarks to tell us where we are and what we should do regarding our child. With it, we have indicators of where we are, where the child is, and what to do in all areas, including discipline. Only with this foundation do we have a cornerstone on which to build our expertise in guiding our child and filling his needs on a daily basis. Without a foundation of unconditional love, parenting is a confusing and frustrating burden.'

He goes on to say that we must make sure our children know that we love them by using eye contact, physical contact and focused attention. I highly recommend his book. In fact, I give it as a present to friends who have new babies as I think it will be of more long-lasting use than a babygro'! Our love must be shown in the words we say and the things we do.

Discipline

'Dear children, let us not love with words or tongue, but with actions and in truth' (1 John 3:18). Discipline without love is authoritarian and detrimental to children, whilst love without discipline leads to selfish unhappy adults who will never be satisfied. In fact, I would say that love without discipline is not real love, for God sees it as an essential part of love. He assumes parents will discipline their children and shows why he disciplines us. 'Endure hardship as discipline; God is treating you as sons. For what son is not disciplined by his father? If you are not disciplined (and everyone undergoes discipline), then you are illegitimate children and not true sons. Moreover, we have all had human fathers who disciplined us and we respected them for it. How much more should we submit to the Father of our spirits and live! Our fathers disciplined us for a little while as they thought best; but God disciplines us for our good, that we may share in his holiness. No discipline seems pleasant at the time, but painful. Later on, however, it produces a harvest of righteousness and peace for those who have been trained by it' (Hebrews 12:7-11).

It may be that the lack of discipline in most families in Britain today accounts for the lack of respect children have for their parents. This is not the reason given by sociologists who tell us to, 'Let your children do what they like and they will love and respect you for it'. This does not seem to be the effect of their philosophy - ask any teacher. They have to try to teach children who have been allowed this so-called freedom. I am sure that it is partly as a result of this kind of thinking that in our society we now have more rules than ever. It is interesting to note that the writer to the Hebrews suggests that people will have difficulty being Christians if they have not been disciplined as children because they will not understand God's ways.

Of course discipline, divine or parental, is not limited to punishment. As Dr James Dobson says in *The New Dare to Discipline* (earlier editions were called *Dare to Discipline*), 'Children need also to be taught *self*-discipline and responsible behaviour. They need assistance in learning how to face the challenge and obligations of living. They must learn the art of self-control. They should be equipped with the personal strength needed to meet the demands imposed on them by their school, peer group, and later adult responsibilities.' He contends that if we *dare to discipline* then we will give our children these strengths.

As Dobson and Campbell are the two authors who have helped us most in bringing up our children, I recommend reading the above books and others by them. Our teenager is at present finding one of Dobson's books for his age group very helpful. He keeps dipping into it for advice. I know it is a good book because when I make a suggestion in response to a query, my son says, 'That's what James Dobson says.' He must be right!

Bringing up children in the faith

In Ephesians 6:4, God teaches us, 'Fathers (and this applies to mothers too), do not exasperate your children; instead, bring them up in the training and instruction of the Lord'. In Deuteronomy 6:4-7, he says, 'Hear, O Israel: The Lord our God, the Lord is one. Love the Lord your God with all your heart and with all your soul and with all your strength. These commandments that I give you today are to be upon your hearts. Impress them on your children. Talk about them when you sit at home and when you walk along the road, when you lie down and when you get up.' People say that clergy children have a high risk of rebelling and not carrying on in the faith of their parents. Of course, ultimately our children are individuals, accountable to God for their own response, but surely our best way of bringing them up is to follow the Word of God.

We must LIVE our faith. Our children know us through and through. Studies have shown that the main reason young people give for not carrying on in the faith they were brought up in is hypocrisy. Our sons and daughters live with us for at least eighteen years. They see how we are in church and how we are at home with them. They know if we sanction little lies, ignore the laws of the road, insult members of the congregation behind their backs, or don't apply the Word we teach in church to our own lives.

In the journal *Evangel*, Don Carson talks about how his parents' joint Christian lives had an impact on their children. 'It was very difficult to get them to contradict each other, even though we children often did our best to drive a wedge between them, as children do, in the hope we could get our own way. ... They pulled together in family discipline, avoided favouritism, and thereby made the home a secure and consistent shelter. ... We grew up seeing Christianity at work. My parents weren't perfect; but more important they weren't hypocrites. They did not simply talk about the Lord, they put their faith to work ... they could not and doubtless would not shield us from the drunks who occasionally came to our table, from the difficult family situations with which they sometimes had to deal. ... One of my most powerful memories concerns a Sunday morning when Dad had preached an evangelistic sermon in the church. After that service a curious little son crept up to the study door looking for his Daddy, only to discover him weeping and praying for some of the people to whom he had just preached. If in later years I had to learn to struggle with large questions of doubt and faith, truth and revelation, obedience and world view, at least I was never burdened with a heritage of parental hypocrisy. My parents' faith was genuine and self-consistent; and there are few factors more important in the rearing and nurturing of children in a Christian home than this one.'

If we LIVE our faith and talk about it naturally our children will learn how it affects daily life. When they have troubles at school, we'll teach them to talk to God about it as a matter of course. When they have a need, we'll teach them to ask God to meet it according to his will. We'll teach them how to read the Bible and pray each day. At first we prayed over our babies in their cots. As soon as they were able to appreciate books, we read Bible stories to them. There are some lovely toddler Bibles around now and little ones love to have their own. We prayed simple prayers with them after asking what they wanted to pray for. To start with they were thank you prayers, but they became more varied as the children grew older. Gradually they started to say some of the prayers themselves and eventually they could pray without any help. It is wonderful to hear little ones praying from the heart. My group of 3-5-year olds pray aloud in our prayer time at Scramblers (Sunday group) and put many adults in the congregation to shame who won't pray aloud in prayer meetings. These children will grow up praying quite naturally.

Then we move on to published Bible notes, of which you should find a variety at your local Christian bookshop. First of all we did the notes with the children, but eventually they wanted to be independent and read them by themselves. By then they had a wonderful habit of spending time alone with God each day. As their lives become full of activity, young people may sometimes need reminding to read their Bibles and pray, but our example will speak volumes. Don't be afraid to ask them to give you peace for a bit while you have your quiet time. Suzannah Wesley used to put her apron over her head when she was praying and the children knew to leave her alone. What her children learnt from her led them to be used by God in wonderful ways. You don't know how God may be planning to use your children.

Let them share what God is doing in your life. Tell them when God has wonderfully answered your prayer. An example of how Philip and I were able to share in experiencing God's hand at work occurred two years ago when we were having a mission at church. We had all been asked to invite people along to the various meetings. The trouble is that most of the people I know are Christians because I don't get much opportunity to meet non -Christians (perhaps I should create some opportunities, but time is a difficulty). So I had been praying for the mother of one of Philip's friends. I no longer have the opportunity to talk with his friends' parents in the way I used to because he is old enough to go and play on his own. The boy had started coming to our children's groups, but only every other Sunday, as with so many children today he goes to see his father alternate weekends. Philip and I went round at Christmas to invite them to the carol service. They were keen, but in the event his mother was ill and they couldn't come. Then we tried again a few weeks later for a special event. She wanted to come and was pleased we had thought of asking her, but she couldn't make it in the end. The time came to invite her to the mission. As I didn't feel I could call round again I left it with God. I know this is a convoluted story, but it is great how God works out all the convolutions. I will continue - we had been distributing special millennium editions of Luke's gospel to every house in the parish, together with an invitation to the Jesus 2000 mission meetings. A young man had phoned up for an extra copy for his friend and so I took one round to his house in the same street as Philip's friend. On the way I met the friend and his mum. She spotted the millennium gospel in my hand and said thank you for hers. Here was the opportunity I had been praying for – no flash in the sky, just an ordinary conversation sent by God. I asked if she would like to come to any of the special meetings we were having the following week and said that if she did, her son could come and play with mine while she went. It turned out she hadn't even noticed the invitation in the envelope (quick mental note to pray that people would find it), but she would go home and have a look. Later that evening her son came round to play, saying, 'My mum wants to come to the Thursday meeting and can I come and play during it?' What a wonderful answer to prayer! As soon as I could I shared it all with Philip and we praised God together. It has spurred him on to keep on praying for his friend and family. It was all good for his spiritual upbringing and far more effective than a talk on the subject would have been.

God and money

Show your children whom you serve – God or money – by the way you speak about money and how you spend it and give it away.

Richard Forster in his book, *Money, Sex and Power,* says that consciously or not we *will* teach our children about money: 'Our very reluctance teaches. Who we are and the daily transactions of life form the content of our teaching. Our children will pick up from us an all-pervasive attitude towards money.

Should I fear money?
Should I love money?
Should I respect money?
Should I hate money?
Should I use money?
Should I borrow money?
Should I budget money?
Should I sacrifice everything for money?

All these questions and more are answered for our children as they watch us.....

If we are free from the love of money, our children will know it. If apprehension is our automatic response to money, we will teach them worry and fear. Children need instruction in both the dark side and the light side of money. Without this, teaching them how to make a budget and write cheques is of little value.'

We teach our children how to make decisions, again by our example, helping them to know God's will by being steeped in his Word and teaching them how to pray over difficult choices. If there is a big decision to be made that affects all the family

we should have a family prayer time about
it. Some families have regular prayer times
together, but we have never managed to keep
that up. We have on occasion had a time of
open prayer, such as on holiday or when
there is a special need. Melvin or I pray at
breakfast, committing the day to God, and
we say grace before meals. When we found
that grace was becoming shorter and shorter,
we devised a way to make ourselves think a
bit more carefully. The person who prays
(we take it in turns) thinks of something else
to pray about apart from, 'Thank you Jesus
for our food' (which was entirely appropriate
when they were little). Now we have a
church prayer diary that we use at one
mealtime. This is good because it involves
the children in praying for aspects of the life
of the church here and beyond. Ways have
to be found continually to inject freshness
into our prayers because sadly we bore so
easily.

Discussion lunches

Parents need to be prepared to discuss issues
with their children as they grow older,
perhaps topics that have come up at school
or on television. We often have Radio 4 news
programmes playing while we are at table
and that gives many a chance to talk about

topical questions. A few years ago, when the children were aged about five, nine and thirteen, we were privileged to go to L'Abri Hampshire. There everyone eats together over what they call discussion lunches. A topic is raised and everyone at the table discusses it, from a Christian point of view, of course. We all enjoyed it and the children, including our 5-year-old, asked us to have discussion lunches at home. It is a wonderful way to teach biblical truths and to get them to think biblically. Not only does that teach our children scriptural views, but shows them how to work things out in a Christian way.

Outside influence is important too, especially in teenage years. Hopefully, if your husband is the minister, you can ensure that there is good children's work at your church for your children. You may end up doing it yourself for a while, but since worthwhile youth work is essential to attract families in, then no doubt it will be a priority to get that going according to God's provision. I have found that my teenagers will take advice from their youth leader but not from us—even if it is exactly the same advice! I have to admit to sometimes asking youth leaders to reinforce some wisdom I am desperately trying to get across.

If your situation does not allow for good children's work where you are, you might have to work out some alternative provision for your own offspring. For instance, when Melvin was a university chaplain, there were not enough children to make viable Sunday groups at the chapel where he helped lead services with the free church chaplain. Because Christopher was nine years old and coming to the age when many boys drop out of Sunday school, we were concerned for him. We decided that I would take the children 6 miles to the nearest evangelical church with a good children's work. It was obviously a drag getting there and I would have preferred worshipping with my husband on Sundays, but I am glad I did it. I have no regrets and my son is now a fine Christian young man.

Worthwhile sacrifice

Bringing up our children in love, discipline and the faith will involve sacrifice for us, but we must do it. I have recently been struck by the numbers of mothers and fathers, both on the media and ones I have met, who have said they didn't appreciate how much having a child disrupts a couple's life. I don't think any of us quite realise what a difference that little bundle of joy will make. Some people seem to think that they can carry on doing much the same activities as they did before they had children. Of course that is not possible for both parents. The little one needs 24-hour care and attention. It is not just a matter of providing for physical needs.

Don Carson's book *A Call to Spiritual Reformation* would be brilliant for anyone wanting to improve her prayer life. But beware, it is very challenging. In his exposition of Paul's prayer in Colossians 1:3-12, Carson suggests that not only should we petition God in times of need, but follow Paul's example in praying for more signs of grace in the lives of believers, having given thanks for what we have already seen. He asks, 'Are we as eager to intercede for our own children when they seem to be making good progress in faith as we are when they are succumbing to the influences of ill-chosen friends?' I think the message is pray, pray, pray. After that it is between them and God; responsible human beings and a gracious, sovereign God.

Children of the clergy

Sometimes children of the clergy experience difficulties at school when their peers have unreal expectations, for instance, that they will be perfectly behaved and unusually intelligent. This can be reinforced by their friends' parents. We were walking home from

school once when the mother of other
children walking with us made the comment,
'It's because he is the curate's son'. Whatever
the incident was I could see no connection
whatsoever with whose son he was, but she
was passing on her peculiar concepts to her
children without even realising it. It is not
easy for children to be so identified with their
father all the time. If their dad does the
school assemblies he has a heavy
responsibility to do a good job or his children
will take the flack! At times Philip has been
fed up with other pupils going on about his
father being a vicar and telling him he is
going to be one too. Whilst at our church
primary school, he was called names for
being a Christian and taken advantage of
because his contemporaries knew he would
not hit back. We have used the school's
disciplinary procedures and helped our son
cope by praying with and for him, knowing
that God has power to act. We also pointed
him to Bible teaching showing how Jesus
and his followers also suffered because of
people's hostility.

It is hard to watch our children go through
difficult times and the temptation is to wish
that we could whisk them away somewhere,
or that their father's position wasn't so
public. However, God will use all these
events in their lives to make them into godly

men and women. We must not be afraid if we truly believe in a sovereign God. Don Carson says in his book *How long Oh Lord?*

'I look at my children, and I wish for them enough opposition to make them strong, enough insults to make them choose, enough hard decisions to make them see that following Jesus brings with it a cost – a cost eminently worth it, but still a cost.'

Even so, there can be advantages in being a P. K. (Preacher's Kid). When asked if there was anything good about living in the vicarage, Philip said that you get a big garden which is good for playing football! Christopher said when he was at secondary school that it was easier being a Christian when you were the vicar's son because the other children expected you to be religious. In fact, after a year or two, both children and a teacher came to him with problems as varied as ghosts, conception and birth of babies. They knew they would get a sympathetic hearing and a spiritual dimension on their thoughts. People are hungry for this which is not surprising as we are spiritual beings made in the image of God.

Michael says that being a vicar's son gives him great opportunities to evangelise. When he was five, he knew exactly who in his class believed in God and who did not. He came home one day, very frustrated because one of his friends wouldn't believe in God. 'I've told him he'll go to hell if he doesn't, but he won't do it'. At seven, he reacted to an exercise to invent any kind of machine by drawing a machine that made people become Christians. His teacher asked, 'But what if people don't want to become Christians?' Michael's response was to go back to the drawing board and add a bit to make people want to become Christians! Now he is eighteen, he takes every opportunity to point people to Christ. For instance, when a friend thought Melvin was a priest, Michael explained that he wasn't, and that Jesus is the great High Priest through whom we can approach God directly. The National Curriculum requires children to look at the Christian church and its clergy and rites. My boys have enjoyed telling their teachers that their dad doesn't wear funny garb and, no, we don't have all that ritual in our church or believe those things because they are not in the Bible .... and their teachers could not argue because they were after all, sons of the vicar and they should know!

Dr Ross Campbell in his book *How to really know your child*, talks about the dangers of strictly imposing an expectation of perfection either because of outside pressure or because that is what we think is right. 'An obvious example of parents who think they should raise perfect children is church leaders, especially clergy. We have all heard of the 'preacher's kid' syndrome. These poor people think they must do everything perfectly and allow no one to see a flaw in their family structure - after all they are teachers of the Word of God. Children living in this kind of atmosphere really suffer. They are pressurized by their parents to lead strict spiritual lives, and their peers and the community exert more pressure on them. 25 percenters in the homes of Christian leaders can be damaged by feelings of guilt and suppressed anger, while the open rebellion of the 75 percenters can be spectacular indeed.' N.B. 25 percenters are children who by nature want to please and 75 percenters are children who by nature resent authority. Do read the book if you want more insight into a fascinating and useful observation of different character types.

We all naturally want to do the best for our children. I am sure though, that if we as parents are extra aware of what is going on in our children's lives and ready to help them through and teach them how to cope Christianly, then they will not only emerge undamaged, but actually be stronger to face life with Jesus by their side.

Education

Our children's education is a concern for all caring parents, and Christians will want a good moral and all round education for their children as well as suitable academic standards. We will have differing views on private versus state education, but the concern for ministers' families seeking state education is that we generally have to live where the church is, and this might mean than our children don't get into the most suitable schools for them. Also we will probably have to move during their progress through school and at stages that do not seem ideal.

We have met these problems. Christopher, now a graduate with a good degree from Durham University, attended six schools from the ages of five to eighteen. This included a move between years ten and eleven, mid G.S.C.E. courses. When we were praying about that last move, we were aware that God was taking our children into account in his plans as well as Melvin and his ministry. In the event Christopher gained eight good grades and only in one subject did he get a low grade because the course work that he had done in year ten didn't fit the syllabus followed at the new school. God looked after him.

Michael has a very positive outlook on moving schools. He likes a change of scenery and it means he reaches a wider range of people. Changing neighbourhood as well as schools has taught our sons to be adaptable and how to make new friends. They are all very good at noticing the new pupil or the one who doesn't fit in and trying to make them feel wanted. I suppose they are very aware of what it feels like and I am delighted they are so practically caring. Christopher and Philip were preschool age when we lived in areas with very good nursery provision. We had put Michael's name down for a nursery, but God led us away from there. As the next locality had very few nurseries, and we didn't live near any of those that were there, he had to make do with three mornings a week at a play group. It was a good one, but I thought he would have benefited from a half-time nursery place. Michael took longer than the other two to settle into infants' school, but maybe that would have happened anyway. Still, I believe God was in control and later he had no problems about going to school except that it was hard to get him up in the mornings!

We have struggled with choice of secondary school, particularly for Philip, as the school where we now live was bottom of the league tables. Of course league tables don't tell everything. Our local school may have very low pass rates but it does have its successes. However, while we were sure the staff at the school could teach our child such that he reached his full potential academically, he would have found the social atmosphere there quite impossible to cope with given his sensitive nature. We prayed and agonised over the decision. I lay awake at night seeing my son in absolute misery at this school. The reality of the situation here is that there is no effective parental choice. Eventually we decided to go private and see what grants might be available. I slept easier at night with the thought of our finances being stretched to the limit (we have no extra income), than I did at the thought of an unhappy child. In the event, God richly blessed us with grants for the full fees, though we do have to fund all the extras such as uniform and school trips. You may of course have no problem financing school fees, but if you need help try your archdeacon or denominational area manager for church charities and also the Charities Year Book (available at the library and on the Internet). We found a local charity which helps us. They usually only help if there are special reasons for the choice of a private school.

However God chooses to use you, rest assured that he will have taken your children into account too.

3

Housing and Possessions

No choice

When we are young we all have our dreams
of how we would like our adult life to be,
and for many that will include the type of
house we would like to live in. I love the
countryside and, while being brought up in
South West London, I relished the times
when we got out of the suburban sprawl into
the countryside. So I dreamt of being
married to a farmer with an outdoor life and
all the space I wanted; a cosy old farmhouse
with roses round the door and chickens
scratching in the farmyard. What do I end
up with? I'm married to a vicar who needs
to work in a city where there is plenty going
on with plenty of people, to whom the
thought of a slow moving country parish is
anathema! Still, God has been kind. Our
city parish is in the North of England, where

the pace of life is that little bit slower and people still have time for each other. God has also given me a vicarage with a very large garden full of mature trees which, if we shut our ears to the traffic noise and keep our sights within the garden, we could imagine was in the country. I have got my chickens, but I can't have them roaming too freely because of the road and unscrupulous people; and the roses are trying hard to grow up round the door despite the pollution! In God's providence I have some of my dream. Ministers' families living in church housing, however, just have to take what comes with the job and make the best of it.

Contentment

'I am not saying this because I am in need, for I have learned to be content whatever the circumstances. I know what it is to be in need, and I know what it is to have plenty. I have learned the secret of being content in any and every situation, whether well fed or hungry, whether living in plenty or in want. I can do everything through him who gives me strength' (Philippians 4:11-13). Twice Paul says he has had to *learn* contentment. It doesn't come naturally to any of us because we are such selfish individuals who put personal comfort high on our agendas. The last sentence is, I think, the key. It is in *God's* strength that we can find contentment.

As regards living accommodation, I had to *learn* it right at the beginning. Because when we moved to Hertfordshire we couldn't afford to buy a house on Melvin's starting salary as a teacher, we rented a council house. It was a lovely three-bedroomed semi with central heating and a large garden. BUT, when we went to theological college, we were given a small damp basement flat to live in. I had to learn contentment quickly or else become bitter and spend a resentful three years. The flat was so small that, in the 1981 census, it only counted as having three rooms. The kitchen didn't count because it was too small! I am a keen botanist, but I wasn't keen on the varieties of mould growing up the walls and slugs in the hallway - ugh, ugh, ugh! The wood lice I could cope with (the toddler next door used to collect them in a jam jar), but slugs - NO!

However, we swapped our draw-leaf table for a drop-leaf one, and used the main room to live in when it wasn't a dining room. The college eventually damp-proofed our young son's bedroom and put a gas heater in. It was a relief to be rid of the smell of the paraffin heater, the use of which only served to make the damp problem worse, but he needed some heat. We managed by trying

to be positive. The one good thing about
the flat was that we had the garden because
the tenants of the other flats had no access
unless they jumped out of their windows!
While there was not much room in the flat,
when it was fine our toddler spent hours in
the garden digging holes - maybe they helped
the drainage. 'Necessity is the mother of
invention', so the saying goes. It certainly
was for me. I rigged up indoor washing lines
and devised a way to get a pram down the
steps to the front door - we were below
ground level. It must have looked
interesting, but it worked. After I planted
primulas in the front area, (it wouldn't be
right to call it a garden) when we were sitting
at the table we looked out of the living room
window to a little bit of beauty at eye level -
and we tried to ignore the dustbins behind
the flowers.

Making a house a home

Edith Schaeffer's book, *Hidden Art*, has been
a great inspiration to me, especially in the
early years of our marriage when we lived in
some grotty places. She writes, 'I am sure
that there is no place in the world where your
message would not be enhanced by your
making the place (whether tiny or large, a
hut or a palace) orderly, artistic and beautiful

with some form of creativity, some form of "art". It goes without saying, too, that "The Environment", which is *you*, should be an environment which speaks of the wonder of the Creator who made you.'

I don't feel that I am an 'arty' type, but I am inspired by Edith when she talks about art as being an expression of individuality, personality and originality, which anyone can do. She encourages us to create an environment in every part of our homes - bedroom, bathroom, kitchen as well as the more obvious areas. I think it is true to say that women especially have a great influence on the atmosphere in the home and thus affect the whole family. You may have noticed that how you feel affects everyone else in the house. I can remember one evening when I was particularly tired, trying to coax a reluctant small child to get ready for bed. I knew it would be best to play games with the washing and teeth-cleaning routine and that if I did he would get to bed happy and relaxed. But I just didn't have the energy and I shouted instead. What a different effect that had on us all. He went to bed crying and unhappy and I felt even worse with guilt added to my tiredness. It sounds like an enormous responsibility that the atmosphere in our homes is so affected by how we, as the woman in the house, are, but we must not forget that we have the power of the almighty God there to help us in the person of the Holy Spirit.

Large houses

When looking at where to go next after college, a vicar showed us the curate's house and apologised for how small it was. We thought it was wonderful – it was above ground, light and airy! Having taught me to accept whatever he gave me, God was overwhelming in his generosity and we moved into a four-bedroomed detached house with adjoining garage. A measure of how our houses have become bigger since then is our living room carpet from the flat which has moved with us. First it went into our bedroom, then in the next house into the spare bedroom, and it would be a mere hearth rug in the large Victorian vicarage we inhabit now. It is difficult now to think how we fitted into that flat, but we did. I believe that God takes our families into account when he calls our men to a particular place and we *will* manage. More than that, we can be content and praise God for what we have. Of course, it makes a difference whom we compare ourselves with. There are always families living in better situations than we are and there are always families living in worse.

That comparison does make me feel guilty at times and richly blessed (which of course I am), when there are those around me who could do with my large house. At one of our appointments we had a spacious home with nearly an acre of garden. My friend lived down the road with her husband and five children in a tiny council house and with no hope of ever getting anything bigger. She managed marvellously, but it made me appreciate what God had given me. Christopher, then aged about seven, was taunted by his school friends who mostly lived in small terraced houses. They said, 'You must be rich to live in a big house like that'. He told them his dad wasn't rich, but God was, and he had given it to us! It can be a problem living in a large house which, if you had bought it, you would have had an income to fit it. However, most ministers' stipends are insufficient for such expenses as large carpets, curtains and huge heating bills. If this is the case for you, it may be worth trying to get your church to understand your difficulties. They might be able and willing to help.

Public use of your house

Depending on the situation at your church, people may expect to use your home for church meetings. Some think that there should be no such expectation. However, you may feel that it is necessary for the ministry of the church for your house to be used. This, of course should be by careful negotiation and be limited to what you and your family can cope with. A few people have no problem having a literal open house with the front door always open for anyone to come in whenever they want. It must, however, be your decision. Unless you are really called to make the sacrifice, such as missionary families living in a culture where it would be seen as very rude not to, and would therefore hinder the gospel work, then I don't think you should have to do it if you would find the arrangement impossible to live with. As always the question to ask is. 'How will my gospel work be best served?' If it would cause unbearable strain on your family relationships, then your work would inevitably suffer. We must find the way of life within which we can function best. For instance, we have always felt that upstairs is private. The children take their friends up to their bedrooms, but that is by invitation. We have a downstairs toilet for visitors. When there has been a queue I have been tempted to let them go upstairs, but then have thought better of it. I think we need some privacy.

In our present situation we are short of rooms for the Sunday children's work which we think is so vital. For that reason the eleven to fourteen-year-olds meet in our house. Often one of our own children has been a member of the group which I feel happier about because they keep an eye on what is going on. We take risks opening our home unsupervised to the congregation, but maybe that is something we are called to do. I haven't held back though, from asking them to take reasonable care of our home, and asking the leaders to watch for chewers after I found chewing gum under a chair, and restricting them to one room rather than allowing them to spread throughout the house. I don't think it's unreasonable to ask the church for assistance with expenses such as heating bills if they are using your home for meetings. After all they would have to pay if they were using the church hall.

I am not one for housework and I would far rather be out in the garden than dusting. Dusting is so unproductive as the dust just gathers again, whereas I can see the plants growing! One advantage of having meetings in our house is that it makes me keep areas of it tidy. It does serve as an incentive knowing that people are going to be using the front room for a meeting! Another plus about having meetings in your home is that if you have small children asleep in the evenings, whichever of you is leading the meeting can also baby-sit, leaving the other free to go out. This also works during the day. If your husband is working at home and there is a baby soundly asleep in his cot, then it is possible to slip out to the shops unencumbered.

Occasionally people seem to have a problem regarding our home and garden as private living space. Some years ago our front fence was taken down as the council was widening the pavement. The wooden panels were left lying just inside our garden and the pile appeared to be getting smaller. Then we noticed a man helping himself to the wood. When we spoke to him, he explained that he was taking it for his brother's fire! Well, the vicarage belongs to the village, doesn't it? Our present vicarage adjoins the churchyard and at the front there was no fence, only a gate around the side of the house. One day I was in the garden when a teenage boy and girl came wandering round the side of the house having an argument. It just seemed to them to be a public place to wander about in, although if they had thought about it, it was obviously not part of the churchyard. A friend of mine lived in a parish where the congregation built them a new house. The people had helped to decorate etc.. But after they had moved in people continued to drift in if a door was left open and wander round the house to see how it looked!

Materialism

We may come from families where our parents could afford to buy almost anything we needed or even wanted, but unless we have full-time paid employment or have some unearned income, we may not be able to be 'kept in the manner to which we have been accustomed'. Or we may just feel that we want to be like everyone else in our society. As ministers' wives, however, we may have to sacrifice the dream of matching furniture and furnishings, kitchen and tableware, or whatever it is that *everybody* has in their home. If this bothers us then maybe we could ask ourselves a few questions. Who are these particular household items for? Who needs them to be matching or of the latest fashion? Not just clothes go in fashions nowadays in our materialistic society. Why am I bothered? Does it hinder my obedience to Christ e.g. in offering hospitality because I am embarrassed that my possessions are not *right*? The items may be nice, but are they necessary for gospel work? If we are troubled by our answers then may I suggest that we talk to God about it and maybe surrender these needs to him and ask for contentment in serving him within his loving provision.

Delayed self-gratification is an idea alien to our contemporaries. Everybody tells us we must have it now. Children are brought up with the notion that whatever they want they can have - including a choice of whether or not to go to church with their parent(s). Banks continually offer loans and shops credit cards. There is a whole industry insisting that we don't have to wait for anything. Ironically, in all this we are denying ourselves! We have lost the pleasure of receiving something we have waited for; saved or worked hard for. Just think how children take for granted a bag of crisps at the school gate or sweets on the way home every day. Compare that with the pleasure of a treat of a bar of chocolate on Fridays or ice cream only on holiday. Delayed self-gratification actually leads to more pleasure. The devil's lie is that we can be satisfied. The truth is that we can never be satisfied, we will always want more. We are like children in the nursery, continually screaming for what we want, now!

Without extra income we cannot hope to keep up with our society's materialistic aspirations whether it be the house, its contents, our clothes, social life, holidays or whatever. But perhaps that's a good thing because we can show the people around us that there is another way, an everlasting way which is richer by far; that relationships are what we should be investing in, not things that will rot. 'Do not store up for yourselves treasures on earth, where moth and rust destroy, and where thieves break in and steal. But store up for yourselves treasures in heaven, where moth and rust do not destroy, and where thieves do not break in and steal. For where your treasure is, there your heart will be also' (Matthew 6:19-21). This is a very well known passage of Scripture. It will be obvious to our congregations where our heart is and will be detrimental to our gospel work if it is so clearly in the wrong place.

The following verses are vitally important too. 'The eye is the lamp of the body. If your eyes are good, your whole body will be full of light. But if your eyes are bad, your whole body will be full of darkness. If then the light within you is darkness, how great is that darkness!' (Matthew 6:22-23). It is with our eyes that we see what everyone else has and are tempted to covet. It is quite dramatic how Jesus says that the darkness will be great in us if we allow ourselves to be drawn into the world's way of thinking. 'Save me, O Lord, from lying lips and from deceitful tongues' (Psalm 120:2). Materialism, like all the devil's ploys, has lied to us. It doesn't bring satisfaction. We know that, but if we are not careful, it panders to our desires and seeps into our thinking without us realising. The devil may be wicked, but he is not stupid. He knows that he needs to use subtle ways to lead the Christian astray.

Back to the past

'Too long have I lived among those who hate peace. I am a man of peace; but when I speak, they are of war' (Psalm 120:6-7). The psalmist is saying how difficult it is for him as a man of peace to live among those who are for war. Similarly it is very difficult for us to live as people of relationship with God and others, while those around us live for material acquisition. It would seem that our society's answer to the question of what to do when our income is less than our expenditure, is to increase our income, even if that means sacrificing something else such as time with people. The alternative (and did not Jesus specialise in suggesting the alternative way of life to that of the world?) is to cut expenditure. This is how our ancestors thought, but it brings us back to self denial and that is not popular.

It may seem strange to say this, but let us thank God that he has forced us to go against the trend by limiting our income in order that we can show people a different way. It is not easy to do either, because society teaches us to do things the easy but more expensive way, and we have lost the skills of our mothers and grandmothers to manage on less money. But we can learn afresh and in another chapter I will share some of how I have been able to do it. It is incredible to our western affluent minds to think that not so long ago in this country, and of course today in many parts of the world, one's income covered the essentials of life - food, clothing and basic shelter – with no expectation of having resources left over for the luxuries (everything we could survive without) that we take for granted. All a family's worldly goods could be put on the back of a cart. It makes me feel uneasy to think of the size of the removal van we needed for our possessions when we moved. I feel poor in our society, but when I was privileged to spend a few days in Kenya it made me realise how incredibly rich we really are. 'Do not conform any longer to the pattern of this world, but be transformed by the renewing of your mind' (Romans 12:2).

Simplicity

John Benton in *Christians in a Consumer Culture* puts it well: 'In an age in which the whole direction of people's lives is dominated by climbing the career ladder, acquisition of material goods and never being satisfied, for a Christian to be able to honestly say, "I am fine as I am, I don't need anything," is a tremendous and glorious shock to the non-Christian's system. It is the cutting edge. To be known as an able colleague and yet to have no greater ambition than to be content in God, is so astonishing it makes people sit up.'

Another challenging book which has been out for some time is Roger Forster's *Money, Sex and Power*. He writes that, 'Jesus' call to discipleship in money can be best summed up in the single word *simplicity*. Simplicity seeks to do justice to our Lord's many-faceted teaching about money - light and dark, giving and receiving, trust, contentment, faith.

Simplicity means singleness of heart and singleness of purpose. We have only one desire: to obey Christ in all things. We have only one purpose: to glorify Christ in all things. We have only one use for our money: to advance his kingdom upon the earth....

Simplicity means joy in God's creation. Oscar Wilde once said that people do not value sunsets because they cannot pay for them. Not so for us! We cherish all the free gifts of the good earth: sunset and sunrise, land and sea, colours and beauty everywhere.

Simplicity means contentment and trust. "Have no anxiety about anything" counsels Paul (Philippians 4:6) "Having nothing, and yet possessing everything" (2 Corinthians 6:10). "I have learned in whatever state I am, to be content" (Philippians 4:11). This is the way Paul lived and so do we.

Simplicity means freedom from covetousness. Paul's confession is ours, "I coveted no one's silver or gold" (Acts 20:33).

Simplicity means modesty and temperance in all things. ... Our lives are marked by voluntary abstinence in the midst of extravagant luxury... Our use of resources is always tempered by human need.

Simplicity means to receive material provision gratefully. Through Isaiah God promises, "If you are willing and obedient, you shall eat the good of the land" (Isaiah 1:19). We are not rigid ascetics who cannot abide a land flowing with milk and honey. Rather, we rejoice in these gracious provisions from the heart of God.

Simplicity means using money without abusing money. In the power of the Holy

Spirit we conquer and capture money and put it into service for Christ and his kingdom. We know that wellbeing is not defined by wealth, and so we can hold all things lightly – owning without treasuring, possessing without being possessed.

Simplicity means availability. Freed from the compulsion of ever bigger and ever better, we have the time and energy to respond to human need.

Simplicity means giving joyfully and generously. We give ourselves and we give the product of our life's work.'

4

Work

To work or not to work? Or rather, To earn money or not to earn money?

For all but the incapacitated or the very lazy, to work or not is never a question. My son loves Garfield because he doesn't worry about questions like this, the answer is simple – don't work! We fill our days with useful activities. For the minister's wife there are even more opportunities to serve God in the ministry of the church than for the average Christian wife, because she is right there in the hub of the church's activity. Consequently, what we are really talking about is whether to go into paid employment or not.

Everyone's circumstances are different. There may be just you and your husband in your family or you may have children preschool, at school or post-school. You may be easily employable outside the home or you may not. Everyone's character is different. You may have many practical gifts or you may prefer cerebral activity. You may be very energetic or you may need a less active lifestyle. You may hate the thought of working at home but need somewhere to go every day. You may have a private income so that you are rarely short of funds, or you may find a life restricted by lack of money very difficult to handle. While we are all different, we are all Christians seeking to serve our Lord to the best of our ability. Our overriding question when making decisions must, therefore, always be, 'What will best serve the kingdom?'

My story

I want to share with you my circumstances and how I have thought the issues through and the decisions I have come to in the hope that my thinking will help you decide what is right for you in God's sight. As I have said, I trained as a teacher of three to eight-year-olds. That was what I had always wanted to do. Because I love little children I wanted to work with them. I taught for two years in Hull while Melvin finished his degree and teacher training. Then we moved south for him to get a job. At that time teaching posts were very hard to come by and, as Hertfordshire was taking on no new permanent primary staff (only teachers redeployed within the L.E.A.), I ended up with two temporary posts that year. I taught maths to children with special needs in a secondary school. The school was desperate and I agreed to try it. It is not exaggerating to say that it was the worst term in my life, but it did lead me to pray a lot - an awful lot! They asked me to stay on, but I politely declined!! I managed to find a two-term post as a reception class teacher. So I went to fifteen lovely four to five-year-olds who were keen to learn, full of wonder at the world ... and they were smaller than me!

We had decided to start a family about then and by the time that contract came to an end I was pregnant. Because there was no question of maternity leave as I had no permanent job, I just left to have our baby. The maternity grant was still in existence then and I got the grand sum of £25 which bought a liquidiser in which to make my own baby food. I believe that the grant used to be enough to buy a pram! As Melvin was teaching we had enough to live on. In fact we still felt quite rich after having been students.

That didn't last long, because soon we went to Oxford for Melvin to start his ministerial training. Then we had no income.

The Church of England paid for Melvin, but contributed nothing for families. I didn't really consider going out to work because I wanted to bring up my own child. There wasn't so much pressure then (1980) to be a working mother. Most of my contemporaries left work to care for preschool children and only returned to employment when the children started full-time school. The prevailing climate is quite different now with most mothers seeming to return even while their children are babies by using nurseries and child minders. The comments people make indicate that they feel they have to work in order to keep up with their financial commitments. Mothers don't usually share the exact nature of what they are spending their money on, but I wonder if the sacrifice of entrusting your child in its most formative years to someone else is worth it compared with the sacrifice of having a so-called lower standard of living. That begs the question of how as Christians we should measure 'standard of living'. As we have already seen, relationship to God and others is far, far more important to the Lord.

I appreciate that most people's biggest financial liability is their house and we as church employees are spared that. However, looking at new house building, the trend is for bigger houses with a bedroom for each child – a luxury families always used to manage without. It would be true to say that our western materialistic society generally considers 'doing without' or self-denial as unacceptable if at all possible. I suppose it's true that if I am the centre of my universe then pleasing me is paramount. What I think is the danger for Christians is that we get sucked into this mentality without realising it because it is so all-pervasive in our nation. The children's catch phrase of the moment is very important for us too. Are we always asking ourselves W.W.J.D.? - What Would Jesus Do?

Better off ... or not?

Harry Blamires has some interesting things to say on the family and the status of motherhood over the years in his chapter on the family in his book *The Post Christian Mind*. He says that the full-time job of looking after the young and running the home, 'was not considered a less dignified or worthwhile occupation than going outside the home to work. Indeed, in the interwar period people turned up their noses in sympathetic pity for married women who "had to go out to work"... the general pattern was to treat [womens'] occupations as proper for the yet unmarried or for the widowed .... The crucial difference now, ... is that the norm of married life has ceased to be that of working husband and housebound wife.' Blamires goes on to say that the feminist movement can claim a victory in broadening the career pattern of women, but he doubts whether this transformation of the woman's lot has been in all respects as positive as the feminists claim. He suggests that as households have become two-salaried, the cost of housing, for instance, will have risen in line with available income.

Surveys suggest that women are still not happy with their lot as they still do most of the housework. Husbands often work very long hours and the mother is burdened with the stress and guilt of trying to do two jobs at once – mothering and working for an employer – and doing neither to her own satisfaction. Women want to be equal with men and not many would argue with the notion of equal pay for equal work. Yet we must not confuse equality of standing with identity of function. Blamires asks, 'What is the alternative for a woman who is financially dependent on a husband she has freely chosen to run a household for? There is only one alternative, and that is to be financially dependent on an employer who graciously accepted her supplication for work. Certainly, to be at the beck and call of an employer is not more dignified than running a home for husband and children. The homemaker has all-round advantages in terms of personal freedom. There is no area of experience today in which people are more susceptible to self-deception than in this matter of what constitutes true dignity and freedom in the ordering of responsibilities between husband and wife. Some of the ironies were pointed out decades ago in an earlier phase of the women's movement, when G. K. Chesterton observed that thousands of women had declared, 'We will not be dictated to,' and promptly took up jobs as shorthand typists!'

As Christians, Blamires says, we need to think whether the family pattern we have settled for is Christian or not. He thinks that, 'only by the diminution of Christian principles could we have obtained the present situation - one in which children come home from school to empty homes, where mothers are no longer always there as guides and caregivers, as advisers or consolers, to share the daily ups and downs of young life in sympathy and understanding. Yes, we had a pattern of relationships which the Christian could appreciate and recommend. But that pattern has been destroyed and it has not been replaced. This pattern is in keeping with the gradual post-Christian rejection of those structures and frameworks, social and ethical, that distinguish civilized life from the life of the jungle.' We really do need to think long and hard and biblically about how we are going to arrange our working lives. For a very interesting insight into the damage that secular thinking has caused for women I recommend Kirsten Birkett's book, *The Essence of Feminism.*

Every need supplied

Back to my story. Melvin was at theological college and we had to rely on our friends from our church and on charities for income. It was hard, but very good for us to have to trust God for every penny. When we applied for rent and rate rebates, free milk and vitamins, the council had difficulty with our application because they required evidence of our income. We only had promises of money and they couldn't cope with that. As a result they put us down as having no income! Of course we knew that our heavenly Father would care for us. 'Look at the birds of the air ... your heavenly Father feeds them ... See how the lilies of the field grow. They do not labour or spin. ... So do not worry, saying, "What shall we eat?" or "What shall we drink?" or "What shall we wear?" For the pagans run after all these things, and your heavenly Father knows that you need them. But seek first his kingdom and his righteousness, and all these things will be given to you as well. Therefore do not worry about tomorrow, for tomorrow will worry about itself. Each day has enough trouble of its own' (Matthew 6:26, 28, 31-34). As you would expect, God never let us down. Gifts arrived just when we needed them e.g. the money for a paraffin heater for Christopher's bedroom. Poor little chap, he was so cold in there. Oxford is a damp place at the best of times and below ground level in Oxford is even damper! Many Christians will testify to God's special provision when they have nothing and it was a privilege to experience it. Of course, we must remember that God provides our salaries and stipends too, as all good things come from him.

I went on to have two more children spread out over the years and never considered going out to work while they were small. They needed a full-time carer and that was definitely my role. Motherhood is arguably the most important career and feminism has done a terrible thing in devaluing a mother's role in the home. No doubt there was much wrong with the downgrading of women's abilities and contribution to society in the past, but it seems to me that many have thrown the baby out with the bath water. Sadly, it is children who are paying the price, and society that will suffer as a whole as children who have not had a secure and loving childhood grow up into dysfunctional adults.

Don Carson in *A call to spiritual Reformation* says, 'In some measure ... greed characterises every culture in this fallen world. But the raw worship of Mammon has become so bold, so outrageous, so pervasive in the Western world during the last ten years that many of us are willing to do almost anything - including sacrificing our children - provided we can buy more. So what we need, then, is integrity coupled with generosity, a new freedom from this miserable enslavement to wealth, an enslavement that is corroding our resolve and corrupting our direction.'

Decision time

When our youngest son was coming to the end of his time in nursery school, ready to go to 'big school' (how small it seems now, but *so* big at five!), I thought about returning to work. Firstly, I enjoyed teaching and, secondly, the money would have come in handy. I had decided that full-time teaching was out of the question, because I already had a job as a wife and mother. As teaching really is a full-time job and involves a great deal of work outside the classroom, it is all-consuming of one's energy. Children are very demanding and there is no way a class teacher can relax for one second during the day. Don't ever say that teachers have too much holiday – the job is so intense that no-one could keep it up without the school holidays. It's not the children who need long holidays, it's the teachers!

I went into my sons' primary school on a voluntary basis to see how I felt back in the classroom. I did enjoy it – *but* – I realised that teaching was not the same job I had done in the 1970s. I have never worked with the National Curriculum and the paperwork that goes with it. Also the behaviour of children had deteriorated so much and so many restrictions had been placed on teachers regarding dealing with disciplinary matters. Consequently, I concluded that I would not be able to cope with the job or enjoy it as I used to. Another problem was how to be a primary teacher on a part-time basis. A class of small children needs one individual with them all the time, someone whose ways they can get to know and with whom they can feel secure enough to work hard. This situation does not lend itself to part-time work. I could have done supply teaching, but that is not very satisfactory in terms of developing relationships with children. I was also restricted in the days I could offer without giving up my other commitments and frightened of getting sucked into doing more than I should. I had seen it happen before. For instance, I knew a lady who started doing casual supply work just one or two days a week in a way that did not affect the work she did in the church or the group she attended. Then her employers asked her to do a whole week and she had to miss the group meeting. Then someone was off long term sick and, since she knew the situation and was so good, (and anyway the money was certainly very useful), she worked for longer periods. Soon she stopped attending the Bible Study group and found she had no time to prepare for the Sunday children's group she led and had to give that up too. It was all very subtle, but the net result was to the detriment of her life and the church's. I didn't want to be lured into getting my priorities wrong.

You may have noticed that all our busyness throws up a big problem for the church. There is a great lack of people with time to give to voluntary gospel work -

including the practical needs of keeping the church property in good order. No-one has time even to cut the grass. But most people are not prepared to use their earnings from the employment that prevents them having time, to pay a gardener to do it instead. The church loses out all round.

Time together

Another consideration for me when thinking about taking outside employment was all the things I was doing that I would have to give up if I took a regular job. Specifically, I had to think of the daytime ladies' Bible study and discussion group, the mother and toddler group and a day off with Melvin. That, I think, is of vital importance. Most clergy need to take a day off during the week because of Saturday commitments. When Melvin was a university chaplain it was easy because he could take Saturdays off and be with me and the children – it is no use trying to work with students on a Saturday as they are all in bed! But now in an ordinary church he takes Friday off. We value those times together very much and now all the children are at school we get much appreciated quality time together. If I worked all week we would not get this time together and Melvin would have to have his day off on his own and I am not sure if that would work. I can imagine a golfer or someone with a hobby that he can go off and do on his own relaxing on his day off, but otherwise I fear it would not happen and the man would soon burn out. I am going to look at time off later so we'll leave further discussion of this topic until then, but you see how it impinges on the wife's thoughts about paid employment outside the home. Couples do manage, but I wonder what the price is with regard to their marriage relationship. It must be difficult; it is a risk and unfortunately the statistics put the chance of breakdown as unusually high for clergy marriages.

Of course if I went out to work, although I would have contacts with non-Christians, I would not have time to spend with the people I had contact with whilst I was based at home. I figured that someone else could fill the teaching post, but no-one else could do the work for God that I was doing in the family or in the community. As a result I gave up the idea of going back into teaching and carried on as I was, with less income, but fulfilling the roles I believe God had given me. I continued to be at home when the children came home from school and when they were ill or needed to go for an appointment. Michael never appeared to take much notice of me when he came home, always eager to get on with his playing, but when he was fourteen he told me how much he had appreciated me always being at home for him. He felt secure knowing that I was there. Child psychological studies show that children who feel secure at home feel safe to tackle the frightening world out there. I can remember talking to Christopher once when he was around thirteen or fourteen about his peers at school who were out on the streets in the evening. He said he felt sorry for them because they didn't have homes they wanted to be in so they went out and often got up to mischief. I believe that this is the core problem underlying drug taking, teenage sex and youth crime too. Youngsters are looking for relief from insecurity and insignificance. Drugs make them feel better, sex makes them feel special to someone, and crime either funds their drug taking or gives them excitement. My boys have never felt the need to do any of these things and were, therefore, able to resist the temptations that come every youngster's way. Fortunately there is one hope for these children who have been failed – Jesus Christ, in whom is to be found the ultimate knowledge and sense of security and significance.

Around that time I knew a Christian lady who had problems in her life. She saw a Christian counsellor for a while and in the end she not only sorted her life out but also grew in her Christian faith. I had read Larry Crabb's books on counselling and was very taken with his approach to problems with coping with life, combining counselling insights with the Christian faith. I had counselled women with problems at a Life Pregnancy Care Centre after a certain amount of training, but I sought the Lord's guidance about gaining proper qualifications in order that I could counsel people through their problems to a closer walk with God.

An open door

We moved at that point and I thought that as I had left my mentor behind it would be difficult to carry on with this idea. But God's hand was in it as always and I found there was an evening class entitled 'An introduction to counselling and personal relationships' at the nearby university. I went on the course and then, after a further two years part-time study, gained a diploma in counselling. I have used courses and books to link my secular training in with the Christian faith in order that I can offer a Christian counselling service to members of the church. Melvin obviously appreciates being able to hand over to me people who need more than just a listening ear and I have found it very fulfilling. There are inevitably ups and downs as in any professional occupation, but it is wonderful to see people move on through their problems to a greater maturity in Christ. I don't earn money out of the counselling because I don't want to have to deny anyone help if they can't pay, but there are expenses involved. Fortunately I get my supervision free from a well qualified member of the church, but I have to pay for insurance, professional membership fees and any courses I go on. Therefore I ask my clients, if they have an income, to contribute voluntarily into a counselling fund held by the church from which I can draw when I need to. Hopefully it will fund others to train and counsel too as I would love a colleague. Counselling has been a gift from God to me as it has enabled me to develop personally and professionally while still keeping my priorities of God and family first. The Lord has also blessed me with a lovely way to be involved with teaching children by giving me the opportunity to run the three to five-year-olds Sunday group at church. Consequently my teaching abilities and love of small children are being used too. What a great God we have!

Then one summer, I found myself actually earning some money. My first earnings in twenty-two years (apart from a little I earned whilst on a counselling placement for my diploma) came about like this. We were distinctly lacking funds, having spent more than we ought on a few days away. I had a camera which I bought years ago which was very good but very heavy and bulky compared to the new compact cameras which take good pictures and are much easier to carry around, particularly when rambling in the countryside. As I thought it would be useful to buy one, I sought advice from a camera enthusiast and managed to sell my old camera through the local newspaper for a very good price. Because I would not be purchasing a camera again for many years, I thought it prudent to try and buy the best I could afford. At the time all I had was what I got for my old camera. So I asked God for a little money – just £20 would do – if it was his will. Around that time I attended a clergy wives conference where we were challenged to evangelise as much as we ask our congregations to. I do what I can, but I don't know many non-Christians and it was difficult to think how I might meet any. Then Philip brought home his school newsletter. A new day nursery associated with the school which is just down the road had opened a few months previously and in his newsletter they were asking if anyone would go on a 'bank' for supply work, as and when they were needed. This seemed to be the answer to my prayer. There would be no commitment to working when I didn't want to, no preparation, just being paid to look after other people's small children. I went along and the manager more or less offered me the job on the spot. I said I was a trained teacher and experienced mother of three, and that while my family and other commitments came first I wouldn't mind a bit of work to fit in. I took the application form home to fill in. The section asking for a reference from my last employer was a bit difficult. However, I sorted something out and started work on the Thursday afternoon that week. I decided that whatever I earned in March would be put in my camera fund and then I would see what I could buy. They only paid just above the minimum wage, but it would still be a lot more than I would have had for a camera. Any more I earned I decided I would save in an account for special projects. I already had to be careful to make sure of my priorities when I was asked to work in the school holidays. Although I could have sorted out child care I was firm that I could only work for them if I had no other commitments. The lure of money and being needed is so very great. The other aspect to my answered prayer was that I was also meeting non-Christians and

I tried to use the opportunities presented, though I have to admit that there wasn't time to say much. The only way effective evangelism could take place would be if I saw them socially.

That job lasted for a few months and then I was asked to fill in, while someone was off sick, at the after school kids' club run by church members. I worked for a term on three afternoons a week. I enjoyed getting to know the children from our local schools. As a result I have formed some good relationships for evangelism in the area. Of course the money was useful too. The down side was being tied to those times at work and arranging everything else around them.

After that I didn't go back to the nursery for work because the benefits didn't seem worth the disruption of other activities or the commitment I would need to make to the employer. The money was useful for some specific projects, but I can manage without more. In retrospect, I see that the evangelistic opportunities were severely limited, due to me being employed to work and not chat! Long term relationships could have been formed which might have led on to something more, but the situation didn't allow for that. I have to say that in my circumstances, time to talk with those contacts we have through church has proved more valuable for the gospel.

Thus the situation for me now is that I have no paid employment. I am not tied to an employer, nor am I tied to the kitchen sink as some would describe the life of a 'housewife'. I am free to arrange my activities and my day as I choose within God's will. A conversation I once had graphically illustrates the predominant view of women working in the home as against being in paid employment outside it. I was asked what I did. I am never quite sure how to answer that question in order to convey my meaning, but this time I chose to follow Dianne Parson's idea of saying, 'I am senior care manager at home!' 'Oh,' said the lady, in an interested tone, 'Which home?' 'My home,' I replied, to which she offered another, 'Oh' but this time decidedly disinterested. It seems that to care for children or adults outside of your home is valuable, but to care for one's own dependants doesn't count. This view is far from the attitude we are exhorted to have by the scriptures. I count it a privilege to be free and each day organise my time to suit the needs around me.

The role of the minister's wife

While we have the same God-given role as any wife, there is a special role for the minister's wife – like it or not. She has work to do in this capacity. Some we have mentioned. I think that a minister's wife can be a great asset to him. A bachelor clergyman once told me that he thought he could be of more use unmarried as he could focus entirely on his work and not have to take a wife into account. There is truth in that, but a shared life has benefits too, and some would argue that a couple are twice as much use. A wife can take care of domestic matters leaving her husband free to concentrate on his work, relieving him of going out shopping, loading the washing machine or cooking the meals, which all have to be done in any household. When life is tough, or even when it isn't, a wife is a best friend in whom her man can confide. Issues talked over together can bring extra dimensions to the thinking, excesses can be curbed or stimulation given. 'A trouble shared is a trouble halved' is a truism. We are great believers in sharing everything about our lives except those things which are truly confidential such as my professional counselling. We have learned to keep things between ourselves. It is *so* helpful to have a confidante and to be able to help each other along. It is a difficult life and work we have been called to do and we can do it better together. If you and your husband don't share things already, then I urge you to start doing so. Don't think he has too much on his plate to be bothered by your little troubles. He may temporarily have a lot on, but I wouldn't leave an issue more than a few days before telling him. He is your minister too. Make an appointment to see him, if necessary! I am sure he will want to help because you are his dearly beloved and, after all, if you are out of sorts in any way it will affect him in the long run. Now our children are at school all day, lunch is a precious time for sharing. We used to have to do the talking cuddled up in bed. Whenever you do it, make sure you do do it!

Sometimes you will have to be strong for your husband when his ministry is going through a tough period. Other times he will be strong for you. That is the wonderful nature of the God-given partnership of marriage which matures and deepens the longer you have been together and the more you have lived through. At times, when he has a lot to be dealing with, your husband will need to be able to rely on you getting on with running the home and seeing to the children if you have any. Over the years, although obviously Melvin has taken his responsibilities seriously, I have taken the major role in running the family simply because his job takes up so much time. Whatever may occur we know that I am always there being the anchor for the family. I must admit that this has restricted what I have been able to do with my life, and not only regarding paid employment outside the home but also in terms of leisure activities, or indeed anything I might do. I have always had to take the children's needs into account first. Sometimes I have resented this. Men seem to be so much freer to do what they want when they want, which brings us back to the importance of the role of mothering. When considering the issue of outside employment, the presence of children living at home naturally has a great bearing on our decisions. However, I think the priorities must be the ministry and our marriage and how best we can enhance them. There is always gospel work to be done by those with the time and inclination and we must be able to spend time with our husbands.

Juggling priorities

How do we keep going with all the demands made on us. James Dobson ends his book *Dare to Discipline* with a chapter entitled *A moment for Mom.* He makes some useful suggestions which are relevant to all of us, mothers or not.

1. *Reserve some time for yourself.*
It is important for a mother to put herself on the priority list too. At least once a week she should go bowling or shopping, or simply "waste" an occasional afternoon. It is unhealthy for anyone to work all the time, and the entire family will benefit from her periodic recreation. Even more important is the protection and maintenance of romance in her marriage. A husband and wife should have a date every week or two, leaving the children at home, and even forgetting them for the evening. If the family finances seemingly prohibit such activities, I suggest that the other expenditures be re-examined. It is my belief that money spent on "togetherness" will yield many more benefits than an additional piece of furniture or a newer automobile. A woman finds life much more enjoyable if she knows she is the sweetheart, and not just the wife of her husband.

2. *Don't struggle with things you can't change.*
The first principle of mental health is to learn to accept the inevitable. To do otherwise is

to run with the brakes on ... Life has enough difficult crises in it without magnifying our troubles during good times, yet happiness is often surrendered for insignificant causes. I wonder how many women are miserable today because they do not have something that either wasn't invented or wasn't fashionable just fifty years ago. Men and women should recognise that discontent can become nothing more than a habit – a costly attitude that can rob them of the pleasure of living.

3. *Don't deal with any big problems late at night.*
Fatigue does strange things to human perception. After a hard day of work, the most simple tasks may appear insurmountable. All problems seem more burdensome at night, and the decisions that are reached then may be more emotional than rational. ... Tension and hostility can be avoided by simply delaying important topics until morning. A good night's sleep and a rich cup of coffee can go a long way toward defusing the problem.

4. *Try making a list.*
When the work load gets particularly heavy there is comfort to be found in making a list of the duties to be performed. The

advantages of writing down one's responsibilities are threefold: (1) You know you aren't going to forget anything. (2) You can guarantee that the most important jobs will get done first. Thus if you don't get finished by the end of the day, you will have at least done the items that were most critical. (3) The items are crossed off the list as they are completed, leaving a record of what has been accomplished.'

James Dobson writes at length on his fifth point, *Seek divine assistance.* The gist of what he says is that God cares about your life, marriage and family. He gave them to you. You ought to pray for help in living for him.

5

Keeping On

Perseverance

Our aim presumably is to be able to keep on with our gospel work for many, many years. If we are to do that we must take care of ourselves. God ordained that we should all work for six days and rest on the seventh (Exodus 20:8-11). Society, however, mostly now works for 5 days and has 2 days off, but it is unusual for clergy to be able to do that. What is more, they often work all their waking hours. This level of toil cannot be sustained over a very long period except in exceptional personality types. It is therefore vital that your husband takes adequate time off and I think that we, as ministers' wives, have a very important role in making sure this happens – even to the extent, dare I say it, of nagging! They must see their need for relaxation is for everyone's benefit. Much as they would like to think they are Superman, they are not. Maybe they will learn by their mistakes, and there will be times when we will be able to remind them of the times they missed a day off and then couldn't function well the week after.

Time off

Melvin has learned by his mistakes and we now try to keep the 'Sabbath'– Friday for us. It is not set in stone, and it can't be, but contingency plans are put into action if for some reason he can't have it. Maybe he can take another day off or have two half days which, though not ideal, are better than nothing. The day off should include the evening. If you have preschool children this will be the main input time for your relationship. I know how difficult it can be to get babysitters to enable you to get out. The locals most likely use family as babysistters and it is unlikely that you have family nearby. Also you probably couldn't afford to pay anyone. We have found different solutions in different areas. In a town to which many people had moved from outside the locality there was a church babysitting circle. Fortunately they were very generous in their use of the 'points' because

I found it very difficult to 'pay back' as my husband was out most evenings and, when he was in, the evening was precious and I would want to be in with him. When there are students around they are usually very good for babysitting. A comfy sofa, a television and plenty of food and they are very happy to be in an ordinary home! Maybe members of the youth group would be happy to oblige and sometimes there is a wonderful older lady in the congregation who makes it known that she is happy to help out whenever she can.

My husband feels he can't take Saturday off because, having written his sermon earlier in the week, he likes Saturday morning to go over it and to think about what he will be doing on Sunday. Administration needs to be done and people often contact him on Saturdays as they are not at work. Also there are weddings and meetings such as the monthly men's breakfast. Having done all that he usually takes Saturday afternoon off and this gives him time with the children. There is no need for a minister to feel guilty about taking time off as he is still having less than the average working Briton.

Now you have established your day off, what are you going to do in it? DON'T MOW THE LAWN, unless you enjoy doing it and find it relaxing. Melvin always used to do that but hated having to use up his time off cutting grass. Another disadvantage was that, due to the vagaries of British weather, if it rained one Friday it was another week before he could attempt it again. The trouble was that it grew longer and longer and became more and more difficult to mow. It took more time, was harder work and added to the frustration of having to use his day off to do it anyway! A friend has found the answer – take an hour off during the day sometime in the week (it will take most clergy an hour or more to mow their lawns because they are often so big). Don't feel guilty about it and it will be good for you too because you will be taking some physical exercise – a good antidote to all that sitting and thinking. The garden can be a guilt laden part of a minister's life. A vicar once said to me, 'If I don't keep the garden tidy people comment on what a mess the vicarage garden is, and yet if I'm seen out doing it they want to know why I am not in my study doing what I am paid for'.

So here we are – Friday morning – how are we going to spend the day? Many advocate planning your day off in advance. That is a lovely idea and adds to the enjoyment with anticipation, but it is easier said than done. The week is so busy our minds are not on our day off. The other factor is that we never know what the weather is going to be like. For us, lack of spare cash makes a favourite option a walk in the countryside. That is free, healthy and gets us away from it all. It can be so peaceful if you find a valley where there is no sign of human beings at all. We love people or we wouldn't be in this job, but we need to be alone sometimes. However, a walk in the country is not as pleasurable if it is tipping it down with rain!

An alternative for us in Hull are the free museums although we cannot go more often than they change the exhibitions or it gets a bit boring. We sometimes walk the two miles into the city centre in the rain and go to a coffee shop just for something to do. It does give us an opportunity to talk as we walk along and drink our elevenses. As Melvin loves films, we have been known to go to a lunchtime showing at the cinema, especially when we had to be back by 3 pm for school ending. We take our sandwiches and our flask and watch virtually a private showing. Alternatively, Melvin might watch a film he has recorded from the television, because he is rarely in to watch them on an evening or he is too tired.

Obviously you will have to do what you enjoy – anything but work. Melvin finds it more difficult to relax while we are in the house because it is his workplace too. It can be very hard to keep him out of the study. Some say that you shouldn't talk about the church on your day off. That is very difficult because it is so much part of our lives and Christianity is our lives. We try to keep off contentious issues, and Melvin has stopped reading anything on his day off which might annoy him. I try to ensure that we spend time talking about family issues and doing such things as planning holidays. Compared with my childhood when we went away for our summer holiday and that was all apart from Guide camp, we seem to take a lot of holidays. However, part of the need for that is that we live on the job. This is even more apparent for those of us whose houses adjoin the church building, but even when that's not the case people know where we are and the telephone is a constant interruption.

People have different feelings about answering machines and of course there are mobile phones now as well. We resisted an answering machine for a long time and just ignored the phone if it rang on our day off or while we were eating or suchlike. Then, when we decided that we might be missing something important or a family member phoning, we decided it would be better if the caller could leave a message. Most people, we have found, don't bother. Either they don't like machines or they decide it isn't that important. Whenever I have been tempted to pick up the phone on our day off because we are in and it keeps ringing, it is invariably work and something which could have waited! There are drawbacks though. I know a minister's wife who wouldn't let her husband listen to the messages until the day after his day off because he couldn't resist answering them. However that made it difficult for the family and their friends. For instance, I needed to contact her about shared lifts for their son to Boys' Brigade but couldn't get hold of her. An alternative is for you, the minister's wife, to be a 'front'. I sometimes do that and explain that Melvin is not available. For security reasons I never say that he is out. Of course, with an answering machine you can listen to the messages just to hear if a social call has been made.

What about mobile phones? Clearly they have their uses, but I wonder if a man's ego needs looking at if he thinks he is so indispensable that he needs to be able to be contacted twenty-four hours a day! I can't think that that does anyone any good. Some churches will pay for a separate telephone line to be put in for the family. There are several advantages to this arrangement. Your husband can have an answering machine on the study line for his days off and for family times. Also the family can have use of a phone for incoming and outgoing calls when he is using his for business (and that becomes more useful as the children get older). The bills are quite separate.

In order to have any sort of break when you have a longer time off, unless you are the kind of people who can switch off wherever you are, you will need to leave the house. Going out for whole days, I would suggest, is a minimum if it is impossible for you to get away. Taking a whole day out can feel as though you've been away. There are difficulties with having to go away, of course, particularly when living on a stretched income. As we just cannot afford to stay in hotels, we rely on friends and friends of friends to put us up or lend us their homes while they are away themselves. It is a wonderful fact about being a Christian, that we are part of a wide family whom we trust and with whom we are willing to share. Staying with friends becomes more difficult as our families expand. It is not easy for the average family to put up another family of five or six members. Some buy a caravan which they can park near friends or elsewhere. There are special holiday places for clergy families and grants available to help with summer holidays. Your denomination's area office should be able to help or the Christian press and the Charities Year Book.

Some churches offer their full-time staff the opportunity to have a sabbatical every ten years or so. It must be good for a minister to take an extended period away from the day-to-day business of running a church to recharge his batteries and reflect on his ministry and learn. This allows him to move forward in his faith, skills and abilities. The congregation may have apoplexy at the thought of their clergyman going away but I am sure they can cope and it will probably do everyone good as minister and flock appreciate each other more when they are back together. That should certainly be the case. It's to be hoped that they don't decide they like it better without him! Melvin is overdue a sabbatical, but at the time he was due one we had just moved to a new church and it would have been inappropriate to go away. We are in the process of fixing something up now. Our sons are at suitable stages in their education for Philip and I to go with him at least for some of the time. Of course he doesn't *have* to go away, but, if it's at all possible and you can get the funding, it might add to the benefit.

In conclusion, sufficient and quality time off is essential for prolonged gospel work.

Spiritual welfare

It may seem obvious that the minister must care for his spiritual welfare in order to be able to minister to his flock, but all too easily it is neglected. This is especially true if he works on his own as he will do practically all the preaching and be unable to discuss issues with a colleague. He can be so busy seeing to everybody else's spiritual needs that he neglects his own. As a minister's wife you have a significant role in keeping your husband spiritually healthy. You must keep healthy yourself and encourage him to keep healthy too. He may not have colleagues to talk to about Christianity, but he has you. It may be that you feel inadequate because you haven't had the training or be so well read, but I am sure he would appreciate using you as a sounding board. In any case, it will keep him in touch with the average church member's level of understanding if he talks things over with you!

You can help to make sure he reads. Encourage him to buy or borrow up-to-date well written, sound books and then keep the children out of the way while he reads them. Enable him to go on at least one good teaching conference a year, where he will be taught and recharged to give out for the next year. Melvin has described his attendance at the Evangelical Ministers' Assembly started by Dick Lucas as his 'lucasade', because it gives him energy to keep on! There are several good conferences on offer and your denomination or your church may be able to help with funding. After all, they are going to benefit from a revitalised minister too. People have commented that they can tell when Melvin has just been at a good conference where he has been fed. The energy shows! If your husband has no colleagues, or even if he has, there may be a fraternal of like-minded clergy in your area who meet for fellowship, teaching and prayer every month or so. If there isn't, then perhaps he can set one up and invite people along. The telephone is wonderful for long distance conversations. £1 or £2 is a small price to pay for a chat with a friend who can help him or you get your spiritual thoughts back into perspective.

You need to take care of your spiritual needs too. I know it can be difficult, particularly when you have young children and there is no crèche or children's groups, or one which you have to take a large part in running, but you must take care of yourself. Make sure you have a proper quiet time as often as possible and try to read Christian books too. As your husband should have a good selection on his bookshelves ask him for a recommendation. Reading is easier said than done, you will be saying. I know, but if we are realistic in our targets we can make things happen if we really want to. One year, after a clergy wives' conference, I vowed to try and read a Christian book for at least one hour a week. It has been a good discipline to have it in mind and not feel guilty about sitting down in the day to read. As my evenings are now full of children I have to convince myself that it is not wrong or lazy to be doing it. I haven't always succeeded, by any means, but I have read more than I would have done without the resolution. Some set up reading groups, where they will read an agreed book over a period of time, say one or two months, then meet together to discuss it. This gives an incentive to read good books as well as providing a social time.

You might also get together with like-minded clergy wives in your area. A group of us have started one here. I am told that it is called a soriety as opposed to a fraternal – sounds awful! We just call it our clergy wives' group, and we have invited wives we know in the area whom we think would fit in. Before meeting we circulate copies of a talk on tape. So far they have been talks from conferences, either one of the men's conferences or a clergy wives' one. The latter are, of course, particularly relevant as they were originally given to women like us. We gather once each half term. One person takes on the role of leader for that meeting and, in order to facilitate discussion, she just notes down some main points that have struck her from the talk. We start with refreshments and, while the assorted children are still happy, we pray. Each of us says something about ourselves or our lives for prayer, then we go on to discuss the subject of our tape. I find it a particularly helpful forum because unlike church groups where we are unavoidably limited in what we can share, everyone in the group understands the circumstances in which we live and they are not members of our congregations, thus we are freer to talk in an atmosphere of trust.

I have mentioned that I have been on clergy wives' conferences and I would recommend that you go on something that will refresh you. We need refreshing just as our husbands do. There are a few suitable conferences available. None are perfect, but even if they aren't I find I gain a lot from going away to sit under sound teaching. It also gives me a bit of space to myself to think, pray, read and have fellowship with sisters in Christ. It is difficult arranging the household, and sometimes I wonder if it is worth it, but when I get there my view

changes and I am glad I made the effort.
When I come back home, we all value each
other's contributions to family life a whole
lot more!

A wife of noble character

'A wife of noble character who can
find?
She is worth far more than rubies.
Her husband has full confidence in her
and lacks nothing of value.
She brings him good, not harm, all the
days of her life.
She selects wool and flax and works
with eager hands.
She is like the merchant ships, bringing
her food from afar.
She gets up while it is still dark; she
provides food for her family and
portions for her servant girls.
She considers a field and buys it; out
of her earnings she plants a vineyard.
She sets about her work vigorously; her
arms are strong for her tasks.
She sees that her trading is profitable,
and her lamp does not go out at night.
In her hand she holds the distaff and
grasps the spindle with her fingers.
She opens her arms to the poor and
extends her hands to the needy.

When it snows, she has no fear for her household; for all of them are clothed in scarlet.

She makes coverings for her bed; she is clothed in fine linen and purple.

Her husband is respected at the city gate, where he takes his seat among the elders of the land.

She makes linen garments and sells them, and supplies the merchants with sashes.

She is clothed with strength and dignity; she can laugh at the days to come.

She speaks with wisdom, and faithful instruction is on her tongue.

She watches over the affairs of her household and does not eat the bread of idleness.

Her children arise and call her blessed; her husband also, and he praises her.

"Many women do noble things, but you surpass them all."

Charm is deceptive, and beauty is fleeting; but a woman who fears the LORD is to be praised.

Give her the reward she has earned, and let her works bring her praise at the city gate.'

(Proverbs 31:10-31)

What a beautiful poem about a beautiful person! Sadly some women balk at this passage; feeling totally overwhelmed at its demands they prefer to ignore it. Well, it does seem impossible that any of us could do and be all those things. This is no more impossible, however, than being a Christian who bears the fruit of the Spirit all of the time. 'But the fruit of the Spirit is love, joy, peace, patience, kindness, goodness, faithfulness, gentleness and self control. Against such things there is no law. Those who belong to Christ Jesus have crucified the sinful nature with its passions and desires. Since we live by the Spirit, let us keep in step with the Spirit. Let us not become conceited, provoking and envying each other' (Galatians 5:22-26). The attributes of a good woman are similar to the Spirit's fruit. I see them as characteristics to aim for with the help of a powerful God, rather than a stick with which to beat myself in the sight of a God who sets unattainable standards and then chastises me for not reaching them.

David Atkinson, in his book *The Message of Proverbs*, suggests that, in the passage about the good wife, we can see beyond the wife to these words applying to Wisdom which is elsewhere described as being worth far more than rubies. 'Blessed is the man who finds wisdom ... She is more precious than rubies, nothing you desire can compare with her' (Proverbs 3:13, 15). This is then additionally, 'a demonstration of what the life of Wisdom herself would look like, were she to manage the home ... The Wisdom of God is here expressed in the creativity, responsibility and artistry of managing a home, providing for the needs of others, and taking a stand on the side of the poor.' Nevertheless, the words are quite clearly written about 'a wife of noble character'. We can, therefore, expect God to speak directly through them to us. What might these words be saying to us? Are we to work night and day, without rest making a magnificent achievement-a-minute? Clearly that would be impossible. No-one in the Bible does that. Even Jesus needed to rest.

Atkinson's thoughts are helpful. 'The home includes work with *wool and flax* (13), and there are *servant girls* (15). There is money to buy a *field* and a *vineyard* (16), trade to be managed (18) and charity to be offered to the *poor* (20). There is enough fabric to make the house comfortable and warm (22), as well as make *sashes* for the *merchants* (24). At its centre is *a wife of noble character* (1). She is loving and faithful (12), careful and hard-working (13-15), prudent (16), *strong* (17) and diligent (18). She is generous (20), prepared (21), extravagant in care (22), dignified and good humoured (25). She is wise (26) and watchful (27), and *fears the LORD* (30). No wonder her children bless her and her husband extols her (28-29) and the key people in the neighbourhood speak *her praise* (31)!'

Unpacking the passage in this way makes it all sound so much more possible. As Christian wives these are all things that result from living our lives as described in the New Testament. Of course, we fall short, that is why God planned to forgive us. But, if we aim high, with his help we might make progress. 'I can do everything through him who gives me strength' (Philippians 4:13). Whereas if we aim low that is where we will stay.

6

Retirement

The changes retirement brings

Over the years of a ministry the minister and his wife have a very definite role, whether they want it or not. In this book we have covered various aspects of that life, not least the expectations from others and the pressures that go with our husband's job and our connection to it. There are some aspects of retirement that seem very difficult and we will look at these in this chapter, but there are also some very positive things to look forward to at this time of life and we will come to these too. I am indebted to Margaret Hacking for helping me write this chapter. She and her husband Philip, retired a few years ago having served the Lord for many years at Christ Church, Fulwood, in Sheffield. Her experience will help us look realistically at this phase in the life of a minister and his wife.

Eventually, the time comes to retire. Maybe we will be forced into it by ill health or else the marching years will dictate. The Church of England now encourages their clergy to retire at 65. Other churches may have different policies or none. Where there is no retirement provision made by the church or denomination, a minister may feel constrained by circumstances to stay in the job. Unfortunately, he may be unable to lead the congregation as he should and the gospel work then suffers. Perhaps some generous members of his church could offer to help him retire by giving financial help or whatever is necessary. Sadly, if a man stays on too long his ministry may suffer so much that there is hardly anyone left in the congregation who can help. Retirement provision is a definite advantage of belonging to a denomination.

Assuming we do retire, we lose everything that went with the position we held. There are not many other professions in which the wife has a role that goes with her husband's job. Doctors used to be similar but I think that was more the case when communities were smaller. Maybe the only one now is a Member of Parliament and his/her spouse. Their lives are certainly under public scrutiny, especially by the press, but the wife's role would be less obvious to most people. Depending on how much we were involved with our husband's ministry, the loss will be greater or less. The effect will also differ according to whether or not you have moved away from the congregation and area.

Moving

Margaret Hacking writes, 'Ministers and their wives spend a lot of time, often against their better judgment, giving advice. I have always believed that it is vital to check that I am taking my own advice before I dare to pass it on to others. If this fails then people can easily say "physician heal thyself". But there is one place where my husband and I have found it impossible to heed the advice given to others. It is an obvious truth that in retirement it is wiser to stay put in one's own home and to continue in the church where one has been worshipping over the years. There is nothing worse than the rapid exile to the south coast to perpetuate summer holidays in retirement, forgetting that one partner will die and leave a rather lonely person normally itching to get back where roots have been deeply placed. Yet here a minister and his wife cannot obey their own instructions.

For better or for worse, and certainly not for theological reasons, it has always seemed wise that a minister should not continue in the place of worship where he has been serving the Lord, sometimes for many years. Possibly in the distant future he might quietly reappear in the back pew with his wife. There are obvious common sense reasons for not being in the way with a minister and his wife who have taken over the leadership. It is a personality challenge, rather than a matter of biblical teaching. Indeed, there is much to be said for the opposite from a scriptural view of the church. But as things are, ministers and wives no longer have a spiritual home and must find another. For some the move is a happy one, but for many, including ourselves, this was a painful exercise because we had been part of a community for thirty years and now had to be let loose at a time when it is not quite so easy to make new friends.'

The upheaval of moving house is forced upon most ministers on retirement. Because some nonconformist ministers own their own home they are in the fortunate position of not having to move at all if they don't want to. But there are a very large number of ministers who will have to pack their bags and move out of the vicarage or manse. As you are probably leaving a house you have lived in for many years you will inevitably have accumulated a lot of stuff. The chances are you will be moving into a much smaller property and there is no way all those settees you had for meetings will fit into your retirement home! You may be good at getting rid of things or you may be a bit of a squirrel and find it extremely difficult to deprive yourself of anything in case it comes in useful ... one day! Perhaps giving your surplus to worthy causes (individuals or charities) will help ease the pain. At least someone else will find them useful – and you will be being ecologically sound; better to find another use or user, than to dump.

Then there is the big question – where will you move to? As Margaret said, convention has it in the Church of England that clergy move right away from where they have been ministering. The idea is that the new incumbent will be able to get on with the job, unhindered by the interference of the last vicar and the people will have to learn to relate to him and not the dear old previous one. Have you noticed that wherever you go the last minister was always wonderful though you wouldn't have known it by the moans the people had at the time!? This practice of moving away can have devastating effects on the couple concerned. You may have been in that church for many, many years. Your friends live there, you know the doctor and where the shops that suit you are. Having been familiar in every way with the area, at a time of great change – new roles for both of you and probably a new home – you are expected to cope with the major upheaval of setting up home in a new environment. It becomes more difficult to make friends as you get older. Friendships take years to cultivate, flourish and blossom. Retirement is a difficult time to start afresh.

Because Philip and Margaret Hacking chose to move to another part of the city where they ministered they can retain some of their 'former life'. Margaret has been able to keep her friends, although it is not quite so easy as it was as they used to be round the corner and now they are a car journey away. She is also still attending some groups she belonged to, but they are not regularly attending the church in which they ministered. Margaret has found it easier to stay in groups than Philip. He was always the leader, but she was merely a member. That makes a difference.

She says, 'I believe that the church does need to look at the relationship between a retired minister and his wife and the church from which they retired. Sometimes it is assumed a minister's wife can very easily find fellowship elsewhere. The whole concept of the body of Christ seems to suggest that we do belong to that local manifestation of the church of Christ and that retirement should not mean that we are pulled away from it to try to get grafted into another part of the body, particularly when we are reaching what was once considered the optimum span of life. Some ministers' wives are delighted to be in a place where there is no memory of them and where they have no history. I am exactly the opposite, and I believe that the church would do well to look seriously at how the retired minister's wife can still be part of the church to which she has belonged for such a period of time. Of course there is teaching and fellowship elsewhere in the wider church, but gone is the warmth and security of long established relationships. Happily I have been able to maintain these to a very real degree, because of the wisdom and thoughtfulness of my husband's successor. But it should not be left so much to chance.

I suppose I have to wrestle with the whole issue as to whether I feel I have lost my role and whether I was too concerned about status. I like to think that most of my friendships within the church were not because I was the vicar's wife, but because I was, and am, Margaret Hacking. But inevitably there is an overlap and it is true that suddenly the role disappears. I hope it means that I am more able to exercise a personal ministry and not just as the wife of Philip Hacking. But again it is an issue that has not been discussed enough in the halcyon years of busy activity.'

There are examples of clergy who have stayed around and been a real hindrance to the new minister and to the work of the gospel. They still stand at the door and shake hands at the end of the service. They encourage people who come to them as their minister with their problems and their moans and groans, instead of gently passing them on to their current minister or aiding the new man by helping the congregation to expect and accept new ways. After all, their congregations accepted the changes they made when they came young and enthusiastically all those years ago, surely they can do it again. While it is natural to like the familiarity of old ways the retired couple can be a mixed blessing, either helping or hindering the adjustments needed. It has been known for retired clergy to stay on church councils or equivalent, making sure they keep an eye on what is happening. This is understandable when you have nurtured and loved a congregation through their ups and downs for many years, but it must be resisted by mature Christians.

We put the gospel first, not our own desires. This is not a problem peculiar to retirement, but one we meet throughout our ministry. Every time we move on we have to leave the flock in the hands of someone else – but not leaving them to fate. We believe in a sovereign Lord. They are his children first, and he will not desert them. 'If you, then, though you are evil, know how to give good gifts to your children, how much more will your Father in heaven give good gifts to those who ask him!' (Matthew 7:11). We can, of course, keep on praying for them, but in retirement as throughout our ministry we must leave their earthly care to another.

A minister could, therefore, stay at the church he retired from if he is able to take a back seat. The attitude of the successor and of the congregation would also be important. The latter need to be mature in their handling of the situation and do everything they can to facilitate the new minister in his work and in settling in. The minister himself would need not to feel threatened by the presence of his predecessor, but able to confidently exercise his own style of ministry. It has been suggested that it is easier to retire from a team and stay around, than it is to withdraw from a one-man ministry because the change is more obvious and a team is less likely to feel threatened than an individual. In that case he would be there to help when needed and step back when not. One area in which the retired man and his wife can offer valuable help is in giving the new minister and his wife background information on their people. Histories are often useful to know. As the previous minister's wife you may be able to carry on with the groups you have been involved with, leaving the new wife (if there is one) to concentrate on using her gifts in different areas. It seems that whether you move away or not people will ask ministers to return to take weddings and funerals. That is something he will have to work out between himself and the new minister. It can be difficult. The new man may feel that he cannot fully minister to his new flock if the previous minister is often called in. On the other hand, the congregation feel emotionally attached to you both, as you will to them. The youngsters have grown up with you and the old people know you well and will feel comforted to have you back.

It seems that in order for the minister and his wife to stay on in the same church there would need to be a great deal of understanding and thoughtfulness on the part of the couple themselves, the new minister and the congregation. A compromise may be to move away at first and then come back after several years. However this does not get rid of the problem of being uprooted from all your support networks – friends, fellowship and community – at a time of enormous change in your roles in life. There may, however, be other places where you have friends and could fairly easily fit into a new life. Some go back to the church where they served their curacy or probation. This may well be where you were when your children were small, when it was easy to make friends. Those friends, like you, will have grown older and be retiring, but they may still be in that area. You will know the community and would settle in quicker here than somewhere strange. You may still have family in a place in which one of you grew up, or you may have a house somewhere that you have used for holidays and so have got to know people there. Hopefully somewhere will draw you and that will make the adjustments a little easier.

Personally, I think that a good church nearby (remember that you will probably become frail, which is a difficult thought), where you will feel at home and gain plenty of spiritual nourishment is an essential to bear in mind when choosing where to buy your house. It would be very difficult if your local church were not suitable. While you

are active you still have a lot to offer, and
even when you are not you will want to be
involved in praying for your church and
ministered to by godly people. When you
have decided where to move to, unless you
already own a property there you will have
to start buying a house. For many this will
be the first time. 'First time buyers' are
characterised as newly qualified and perhaps
newly married, with lots of energy and
capacity for change. The retiring couple may
have less of these attributes, but they do have
experience of the world and will be able to
make mature judgments. As the world of
estate agents, mortgages, stamp duty and
surveys may be a very alien one find someone
who knows – professional or friend – to make
the procedure less of a minefield.

You may have financial worries as you go
into retirement. Churches will vary on the
arrangements they make for their retired
clergy. If you are in a denomination
provision should have been made for you and
the Charities Year Book may have charities
that can help. As in all our life, however, we
are brought back to Jesus' faithful words,
where he promises us that in the same way
God cares for the birds and the flowers, he
will look after our needs because he loves us
(see Matthew 6:25-34). What wonderful
words of comfort. Whatever the unknowns

about retirement they are not unknown to God. He will take care of us as he always has. Why should he stop now? Anyway, Jesus may return before we get to retirement and then all the worrying will have been pointless!

In common with others choosing a retirement home you will want to take into account any visitors you would like to come and stay, especially your children and their families. You don't, however, want so big a house that it will be a headache to maintain and clean. House maintenance will be a new issue for most of us. For years we have lived in the houses given to us, whatever they were like, but we didn't have responsibility for leaky roofs or broken boilers. Also the garden should be considered in order that it will suit your needs. Although I don't think I could survive without a garden it would have to be one which, during my active years, I could set up to be eventually more or less self-maintaining for me to enjoy sitting in and looking at when I became inactive. The closeness to amenities such as shops, doctors and public transport would also be a consideration. A house in the middle of nowhere might seem attractive at 65, but it would make life very difficult at 85. Natural inclines and stairs should also be taken into account.

Retirement – a loss and a gain

Margaret expresses her feelings about the experience of retiring, 'Retirement is certainly a very real bereavement, particularly for a minister's wife when it involves moving away from home and neighbourhood. In one sense it is the last bereavement but one. It has become quite a joke in our home that all too often we are planning for what happens when one or other of us has gone to glory. This can become tedious and a sense of humour is necessary. But it has to be and there will be that final bereavement which we all need to face.

The bereavement of retirement is not dissimilar to the bereavement when children leave the family home for the last time. It is true that there is rejoicing when children marry in the Lord to have the joy of having another member, or members, within the family. This calls for grace on the part of the wife and mother particularly, because son-in-law or daughter-in-law may bring new ideas, even when within shared Christian convictions. In our situation, with a son ordained and a daughter married to a vicar, it has an added dimension of challenge. Again we rejoice at the way in which it has worked and the richness of having a different voice heard in Christian matters. Still, a mother has to learn to lose a son and daughter in the biblical sense as they are now joined to wife and husband. When all this is added to the bereavement of retirement, it makes for a very significant moment in life. My husband and I have discovered so many of our contemporaries who are not coping easily and well. Unfortunately, some ministers have become so disillusioned with their work, that retirement brings unalloyed joy, but for most that is not so and we are now having a ministry even at that level of sharing with contemporaries some of the lessons we have been painfully learning together.

There is a motto that my husband will always be perpetuating and which now hangs on the retirement home wall. It runs 'The best is yet to be'. It is one thing to believe that as a Christian and another to live in the light of it, when so many of the good things seem to be in the past. How vital it is to keep spiritually fresh, and to recognise that not only because of the wonder of heaven, but also because of the present working of the Spirit in his church, these rather trite words are wonderfully true.'

Some of the losses of retirement will not be mourned over. Apparently 99% of retiring clergy are glad to be rid of their

P.C.C. or Church Council! I tell my sons that in every job there are parts which one does not like, and that will be true of the minister's job as much as any other. Since, however, our job is so much part of our life, the losses will be felt more deeply. Overnight the sense of significance, of being important in people's lives, becomes a sense of being incidental and insignificant. There might be a feeling of emptiness and pointlessness which could lead to depression if it is not faced and dealt with. If you or your husband are feeling like this I recommend you seek out a trusted friend or a counsellor, preferably a Christian, who can help you work through the meaning of it all and come to a way of coping with life again.

Your new situation may lead you to a greater reliance on God, which can only be a good thing. It will certainly give you time to enjoy life in a way you haven't been able to do for years. There will be time to think, to read non-essential books, to develop relationships, and to relax as you merely attend and participate in services instead of having to take responsibility for them. You will be able to go away at Easter and weekends and have evenings out as often as you wish! Your husband will always be needed to take services if he wants to where there is a shortage of clergy, a sick minister or a vacancy. But what about you: who needs you any more? If you have children and relate well to them, they will still need you. Now you will be freer to go and stay, to have the grandchildren to stay with you – both of you – Grandad as well!

Margaret writes, 'Some ministers and their wives suddenly take up new interests in retirement. Men challenge my husband as to why he does not get involved in golf, or making marmalade, or laying a new garden, or going back to study. I have similar suggestions about joining art classes, bird watching or encouraging my husband to think of a Mediterranean Cruise, which we now apparently deserve because we have served the Lord so long. There is value in this, but all too often it seems to me to be a suggestion that spiritual work is now over and we can enjoy our mellow years fairly unproductively, leaving the continuing work to others. Happily there are still very many positive opportunities in retirement for giving helpful words of experience to younger ministers and wives. Most ministers are only too pleased to hear from those who have served the Lord in the past, with the proviso that the older man and woman are not too embedded in history. I have found that many ministers' wives under pressure have been only too ready to ask questions and listen to answers that come from years of experience. In many ways the job does not change.

Since my husband and I have always believed that it was a shared ministry, this can continue. However it comes with a different package. Most of our lives I have been at the home base with responsibilities for bringing up the children and providing stability when my husband's life was busy and unpredictable. The vicarage was also a place for counselling and sharing with people in need in the parish. Now things are different. Sharing the ministry means a willingness to travel around the country and abroad. It means receiving hospitality more than giving it. There is a richness in this and a very real opportunity to see the church as it really is and not our own little patch with all its joys and sorrows. On the other hand, there is little continuity and no opportunity to see the outcome of one's ministry. It is so different from the settled, happy routine of vicarage life. I am amazed at how many ministers' wives seem to be unsure of their role and unhappy in what they believe it to be. For us it was very different and yet retirement brings its compensations and another dimension to shared ministry.'

You may then, on retirement, still have a role as counsellor and Christian friend, but

it will be in a different context. As we have
seen it could be amongst other ministers'
wives or in a new church. You will have time
– a rare commodity these days – for people
and a wealth of experience of life. Our
society does not tend to value the maturity
and wisdom that older people have gained
over the years. This is a great loss to all of
us, but as Christians we are used to not
following the world's ways. I think, for
instance, that it is very worthwhile to have
ministers' wives conferences (day or
residential) with older wives as hostesses to
help the younger ones through the maze of
ministry. Who better to help? I find it
encouraging to see how God has been with
them through good times and bad, how God
has used very ordinary but faithful people
for his glory. It gives me hope that I can
serve him too, for I have the same God and
he will surely also use me if I keep the faith.

A last word from Margaret, 'I still find I
am happiest when involved in the work of
the kingdom in some way and, therefore, I
do believe that true joy in retirement is not
just the cessation of a busy life, but the
continuation of Christian ministry in a new
dimension and then the pain of retirement
will seem to be worthwhile.'

7

The best job in the world

Gospel work – making disciples and building up the saints – must be the best job in the world because the consequences are of eternal significance. Your contribution to the work directly and indirectly is worth its weight in gold. While you will be working as a Christian woman within the fellowship of God's people, you have an added dimension of supporting the man set apart by God to lead his people – the minister of the sheep. If you have children you will be making another tremendous contribution to the work of the kingdom as you bring them up in the faith, preparing them to take their place in due time in the worldwide church. Christopher said, after having been at university a while, 'What a privilege it is to have been brought up in a Christian home'. He saw what an advantage he had over those whose upbringing missed God out and how God used this to make him a useful tool for the kingdom. Do not underestimate the far reaching effects you will have as you tend you husband and children and do it in his strength and to his glory.

We could not do better than to pray for ourselves as Paul prayed for the Colossians. 'For this reason, since the day we heard about you, we have not stopped praying for you and asking God to fill you with the knowledge of his will through all spiritual wisdom and understanding. And we pray this in order that you may live a life worthy of the Lord and may please him in every way: bearing fruit in every good work, growing in the knowledge of God, being strengthened with all power according to his glorious might so that you may have great endurance and patience, and joyfully giving thanks to the Father, who has qualified you to share in the inheritance of the saints in the kingdom of light. For he has rescued us from the dominion of darkness and brought us into the kingdom of the Son he loves, in whom we have redemption, the forgiveness of sins' (Colossians 1:9-14). What responsibility, yet what power!

Speaking at the Evangelical Ministers' Assembly in 1995, Peter Jenson had something to say to the men about their wives, 'If the spiritual life of the minister is crucial to the good health of the parish, then the spiritual life of his wife is crucial to his own. As ministers virtually married to our congregations it is so fatally easy to lose sight of the one whom God has placed with us. She may be a person of great personal gifts who does an enormous amount around the place, she may be a rather quiet person who doesn't see herself as an upfront person, but her spiritual life is essential for the spiritual life of the minister and hence of the congregation. The sadness in all the debate on women's ministry is the complete invisibility of the minister's wife who has been in the ministry for hundreds of years.' (Not literally for any individual!)

The protestant home, the protestant minister's home, that great rediscovery of the reformation (there was Martin Luther with his Katie leading the way) has been an incalculable blessing to the Christian church down through these hundreds of years. It is something that has been neglected very much in recent years. So much good comes from the minister and the minister's wife, but so too does much harm. The minister's wife may turn to paths of spirituality at odds with the clear note of the gospel. If she does, and she influences her husband, this would have a tremendously crucial effect on his ministry.'

I urge you, therefore, to take your responsibilities under Christ seriously as you live out your life in the minister's home. Go in God's power and not your own and, mistakes notwithstanding, you will be received on the last day with the accolade, 'Well done good and faithful servant!'

8

Practical Ideas

I thought it might be helpful to share some practical ideas on entertaining and managing on a low budget as many of us are called to do. In the previous chapters I have mentioned quite a few ideas. Here are some more.

Making ends meet

Thrift is an old fashioned ideal that I learned in the Girl Guides. Nowadays the same ideas come under the eco-friendly heading. It is acceptable to be caring for the environment and it just so happens that it is also very economical. The first tenet is to reuse everything if at all possible. Obviously this is cheaper than buying new every time. While a greater initial outlay may be needed to ensure lasting quality no more is spent thereafter. Some things require more time and attention, but that is free and can often include relationship time. Using terry nappies rather than disposable ones is an obvious example of saving money and the environment. They even make them in easy-to-use shapes so you won't have to learn to fold them as I did.

We used to go to jumble sales for second-hand clothes but now they don't seem to happen. Instead there are car boot sales. Apart from them mostly appearing to be on Sundays I haven't got on so well with these. Maybe it is the proximity of the vendor, I don't know. The alternative I use now is the charity shop. We have lots of them in Hull and I love browsing round. I suppose you do need time because to get the best out of them you have to keep popping in. Many times there will be nothing there but occasionally there will be just the item you are looking for. I have made some wonderful purchases. Some days my entire outfit is from charity shops. You do need to look carefully at the garment for stains and try it on if you can. If I don't have time for that, and it doesn't fit, I take it back and the £2 it cost me will have been a donation to the charity. We all get clothes from these shops. Michael quite enjoys being given a fiver and going off to see how many garments he can get for it! Of course you can't usually get trendy gear this way which is what the children want as they get older. Our sons had to have items like official football kits for birthdays although they have managed to find shops that sell seconds of that sort of thing which makes them more affordable.

Unfortunately the boys have found themselves teased at school about having second-hand clothing. Children's characters will determine how well they cope with that, though I am not sure why they had to tell their friends. I think they talk quite a bit about where they get their clothes. Once Philip bought a full England kit from his friend. I was a bit concerned because he came home from school saying that his friend wanted to sell his kit for £8. When new it would have been worth £60. The next day I went to school with him in order to check with his friend's mother that it really was all right. I found he was being collected by a childminder. She said that it probably was fine as the boy would have got fed up with it and if he changed his mind in a few weeks his mother would just buy him a new kit. Philip got a bargain! We can help them handle the teasing as we have talked about earlier. It can come for many reasons and our understanding and backing will help enormously.

The local newspaper is a good source of all sorts of second-hand goods. With many people having so much disposable income there are a lot of hardly used items for sale. Two of our boys bought computer games consoles for Christmas through advertisements in the paper. They got much greater value presents than we could afford to buy new. One of them was bought from a bachelor who was moving on to the next model. When Christopher found that his friends were also doing the same thing, he bought games from them at a fraction of the cost. He has the sort of character that doesn't mind if he hasn't got the latest 'whatever'. Others may care more, and we managed to get Philip an up-to-date console. As the games are astronomically expensive he survives by buying from second-hand specialist shops. There is a plentiful supply of them. He tells me that people buy a game, play on it until they have worked right through it and then sell it ready to buy the next one.

If you watch the gardening programmes on television you will know about the trends to have decking, gazebos, exotic plantings etc. Well, I don't garden on a low budget – I garden on a nil budget! That is for the ornamental side of things. I feel I can justify spending money on the edible section because we will be eating the produce. Growing your own is the most cost effective way to eat organic, fresh, local fruit and vegetables. It takes time and effort, but I think it is worth it and it is healthy for me too, being outside and active in the garden.

Home made meals are definitely cheaper and healthier for you and your family. Raw materials such as meat, flour and fat are less expensive to buy separately to make into your own pie, than if you buy one ready made. What is more, you will be able to leave out all the additives that are put in to keep food fresh longer on the shop shelves and you will be able to make it as you like it. For instance, my family don't like lots of pepper in their food and most tinned soups are too peppery for them. If you shop around you will manage even greater savings. I have noticed, for example, that meat is cheaper at the local butcher than at the supermarket and you can buy just the quantity you need and not the standard amount thought up by someone else.

Jam making is a great thing to do too. You may have fruit in your garden, or you may have friends with surplus harvest which they will be only too pleased to find a good home for, or you may enjoy taking the children to a pick-your-own farm for soft fruit. All these will make your jam even cheaper. It is bound to taste better. It keeps for several years and you will never have to buy a jar of artificially coloured, high percentage sugar jam again. It may sound old-fashioned, but so what! Let us be thoughtful about what we reject and what we keep from the 'old days'.

Entertaining

As a minister's wife it is very likely that you will be called on to entertain, and we have already considered some aspects of this. Hopefully we would all feel able to invite a family for a meal as this is a wonderful way to build up relationships and make people valued. Delia Smith's new books *How to Cook* give wonderful basic instruction which will help you from scratch if that is where you are at and are wanting to have a go. I don't think there is any special talent to elementary cooking; it is just practice, not giving up and learning from your mistakes. We are encouraged to welcome people into our homes in the New Testament. 'Offer hospitality to one another without grumbling' (1 Peter 4:9).

Cooking for large numbers is another matter and takes a certain flair for organisation. If you faint with terror at the thought of this, then maybe you could try and help people see that this is not your gift and not to expect it of you. I am sure there will be others in the church who do large-scale catering and enjoy doing it. However, some just love having hoards of people in their homes for meals: others are prepared to do it occasionally. I gave some ideas that I use earlier in the book, but here are a few recipes from Nicola Coombs which she and others have found easy and useful when entertaining more than the average number of guests. They come from various sources, many forgotten, and have been collected together over the years. I use them with Nicola's kind permission.

ATLAS MOUNTAIN SOUP
(Serves 8)
8 oz/225g pre-soaked apricots
4 tablespoons olive oil
4 cloves of garlic, finely chopped
4 teaspoons ground cinnamon
4 teaspoons ground cumin
4 teaspoons paprika
2 lbs/900g lamb or beef mince
8 sticks of celery, cut into 1 in/2.5 cm chunks
2 large green peppers sliced into green rings
2 tins of tomatoes (or 2 lbs/900g of tomatoes sliced roughly)
2 lemons

1 pint/550ml water
2 tablespoons sugar
salt and pepper

Heat oil in a large, heavy saucepan and add garlic and spices. Stir for 1 minute. Add mince and brown over a slightly higher heat. Add apricots, peppers, celery and tomatoes. Shave 20 strips of lemon rind with a potato peeler and add with the lemon juice. Stir in the water. Add sugar, salt and pepper. Simmer for 1-1 ¼ hours with the lid firmly on.

PARSNIP AND APPLE SOUP
(serves 10-12)
2 oz/50g butter
2 onions
4 parsnips
2 medium cooking apples
2 pints/1.1 l vegetable stock
4 tablespoons chopped fresh parsley
1 teaspoon mixed herbs
2 pts/1.1 l milk

Gently saute the vegetables in the oil for 10-15 minutes. Add the stock and herbs. Simmer for 40 minutes. Add the milk, liquidise and reheat.

PEPPERED SMOKED MACKEREL PATE
(serves 8-10)

1 lb/450g smoked mackerel fillets with black peppercorns

3 oz/75g butter, diced

1 tablespoons lemon juice

4 tablespoons horseradish sauce

5 fl oz/150ml single cream or whipping cream, whipped

Remove any skin or bones from the fish and blend in a food processor with the butter, lemon juice and horseradish. Work until smooth and then fold in the cream. Freezes very well.

MOROCCAN LAMB WITH APRICOTS

(serves 12-15)

3 lbs/1.35 kg diced lamb

1½ oz/40g butter

1 lb/450g onions sliced

3 large green peppers, deseeded and sliced

4 tablespoons vinegar

1 level tablespoon turmeric

1 level tablespoon ground ginger

1 level tablespoon mixed spice

2 cloves garlic, crushed

14 oz/400g tin tomatoes

14 oz/400g tin of apricots in syrup

4 round tablespoons raisins

½ pint/275ml stock

grated rind and juice of half a lemon

salt and pepper

2x15oz/425g tins of chick peas, drained

Toss the lamb in the seasoned flour and brown the meat in small batches. Keep the meat warm and gently fry the onions until soft. Add the remaining flour and everything else, except the apricots and chick peas. Return the meat to the casserole and stir well. Gently add the apricots, being careful not to break up the fruit. Put into a pre-heated oven (170 C. 325 F, gas mark 3) for 2 ½ hours. It is best if made the day before and reheated for ¾ hour. Add the chick peas before the final reheating.

Serve with rice and raita (2 cucumbers finely sliced or grated and left to drain in a colander. Mix 1 pint/570ml Greek yoghurt, 1 crushed clove of garlic, 2 large handfuls of mint and generous seasoning. Combine the cucumber and yoghurt mixture shortly before serving.)

CHICKEN WITH CRISPY TOPPING
(serves 8)

8 boneless chicken portions
4 oz/110g butter
1 teaspoon tarragon
2 tablespoons fresh parsley
1 crushed garlic (optional)
8 oz/225g grated cheese
2 small packets of ready salted crisps

Melt the butter and combine all the ingredients except the chicken. Spread this topping over the chicken portions and cook at 180 C/350F/ Mk 4 for 30-40 minutes until the chicken is cooked and the topping is crunchy.

SAUSAGEMEAT BAKE
(serves 10-12)
6 tablespoons oil
4 medium onions
2 lb/900g pork sausagemeat
1 lb/450g breadcrumbs
Rind and juice of 3 large lemons
4 teaspoons of dried herbs
10 oz/275g dried pre-soaked apricots, chopped
2 beaten eggs
salt and pepper
Gently fry the onions in the oil until soft and then thoroughly combine all the other ingredients in a large bowl. Cook in 2 large loaf tins or one large baking tray for 1 ½ hours at 190 C/375 F/Mk5 . 2 tins of chopped tomatoes may be spread over the top ½ hour before the end of cooking.

INDONESIAN CHICKEN
(serves 10-12)
2 lbs/900g cooked chicken diced
2 bananas sliced

12 apples diced

4 tablespoons sliced almonds, grilled or roasted

12 tablespoons mayonnaise

8 tablespoons of cream or evaporated milk

4 tablespoons mango chutney

4 teaspoons curry powder

Mix the cream, mayonnaise, chutney, curry powder and nuts together. Add chicken and fruit and heat through. Serve with rice or potatoes and salad.

Quantities for 100 people!

20 lbs/ 9 kg cooked chicken diced (approx. 80 breasts or 10-12 x 6lb/ 2.7kg chicken)

6 large 750 ml jars mayonnaise

4 x 410g tins evaporated milk

1 x 95g jars mango chutney

20 bananas

120 apples

500g sliced almonds

MINCE PIES WITH ORANGE

(36 pies)

1lb/450g plain flour

6 oz/175g caster sugar

12 oz/350g butter

rind and juice of one large orange

Combine the ingredients to make the pastry in a food processor or by rubbing in.

Wrap the pastry and rest it in the fridge for
1 hour.

1lb/450g mincemeat

8 oz/225g cream cheese

2 oz/50g caster sugar

Mix the filling together and fill pies made
with the orange pastry. Bake the trays of
pies for 25-30 minutes at 200 C/400 F/Mk6.

LEMON BISCUIT CRUMB

(serves 8)

8 oz/225g crushed digestive biscuits

4 oz/110g melted butter

½ pint/275ml double cream

1 small 7oz/200gcan of condensed milk

grated rind of 2 lemons

10 tablespoons of lemon juice

Mix the biscuit crumbs with the butter
and press the mixture to form a shell in a
flan dish. Lightly whip the cream, fold in
the condensed milk, lemon juice and rind.
Beat until smooth and thickened. Pour into
the crumb shell and chill overnight.

LEMON ICE-CREAM

15 fl.oz/425ml of whipping or double
cream

7 oz/200g caster sugar

2 tablespoons cointreau or kirsch or other
flavouring

rind and juice of 2 lemons

Whip the cream and sugar until almost stiff and then whisk in the liqueur and lemons. Put in a freezer-proof container and freeze.

WHOLEMEAL CHEWY CAKE
(48 portions)
12 oz/350g butter
1 lb/450g soft brown sugar
2 eggs
1 lb/450g mixed dried fruit
4 oz/110g oats
12 oz/350g self-raising wholemeal flour
pinch of salt
Melt the butter and put into a large bowl and thoroughly mix in the other ingredients. Pour into a large, lined roasting tin and spread evenly. Bake at 180 C/350F/Mk4 for 50-60 minutes. Cut whilst warm. Freezes well, interlined with baking parchment.

Bibliography

Atkinson, D. *The Message of Proverbs*, IVP, 1996

Birkett, K. *The Essence of Feminism*, Matthias Media, 2000

Blamires, H. *The Post Christian Mind*, Vine Books, 1999

Benton, J. *Christians in a Consumer Culture*, Christian Focus Publications, 1999

Campbell, Dr R. *How to really love your child*, Victor Books, 1978

Carson, D.A. *How long O Lord*, I.V.P, 1984

Carson, D.A. *A Call to Spiritual Reformation*, I.V.P, 1992

Dobson, Dr J. *Dare to Discipline*, Coverdale House Publishers, 1970

Forster, R.J. *Money, Sex and Power*, Hodder and Stoughton. (no date in my copy)

Guiness, Os. *Doubt*, I.V.P., 1973

Schaeffer, E. *Hidden Art*, The Norfolk Press, 1971

Schaeffer, E. *What is a Family*, Hodder and Stoughton, 1975

Wynnejones, P. *Children under Pressure*, Triangle, 1987

Christian Focus Publications publishes biblically accurate books for adults and children. The books in the adult range are published in three imprints.

Christian Heritage contains classic writings from the past.

Christian Focus contains popular works including biographies, commentaries, doctrine, and Christian living.

Mentor focuses on books written at a level suitable for Bible College and seminary students, pastors, and others; the imprint includes commentaries, doctrinal studies, examination of current issues, and church history.

For a free catalogue of all our titles, please write to

Christian Focus Publications, Ltd
Geanies House, Fearn,
Ross-shire, IV20 1TW, Great Britain

For details of our titles visit us on our website

http://www.christianfocus.com